TONY LEWIS ANTHOLOGY 2014–2016

Melissa Chiu, Theaster Gates, Karl Haendel,
Betsy Johnson, and Tony Lewis

HIRSHHORN

WASHINGTON, DC

MOUSSE PUBLISHING

MILAN, ITALY

Tony Lewis: Anthology 2014–2016 *is the debut volume in a new series of publications by the Hirshhorn Museum and Sculpture Garden—the national museum of modern and contemporary art—that focuses upon significant works in the Museum collection.*

HIRSHHORN EYE INSIDE

Look for the Hirshhorn Eye (Hi) icon next to images in this book, scan the image, and unlock unique insights into the work of Tony Lewis.

Just type **hi.si.edu** into your phone's browser (no app download required) and select this book from the list of options.

Hi, the award-winning instant art guide created by the Hirshhorn, lets you access artist and expert videos inside this book and throughout our Museum.

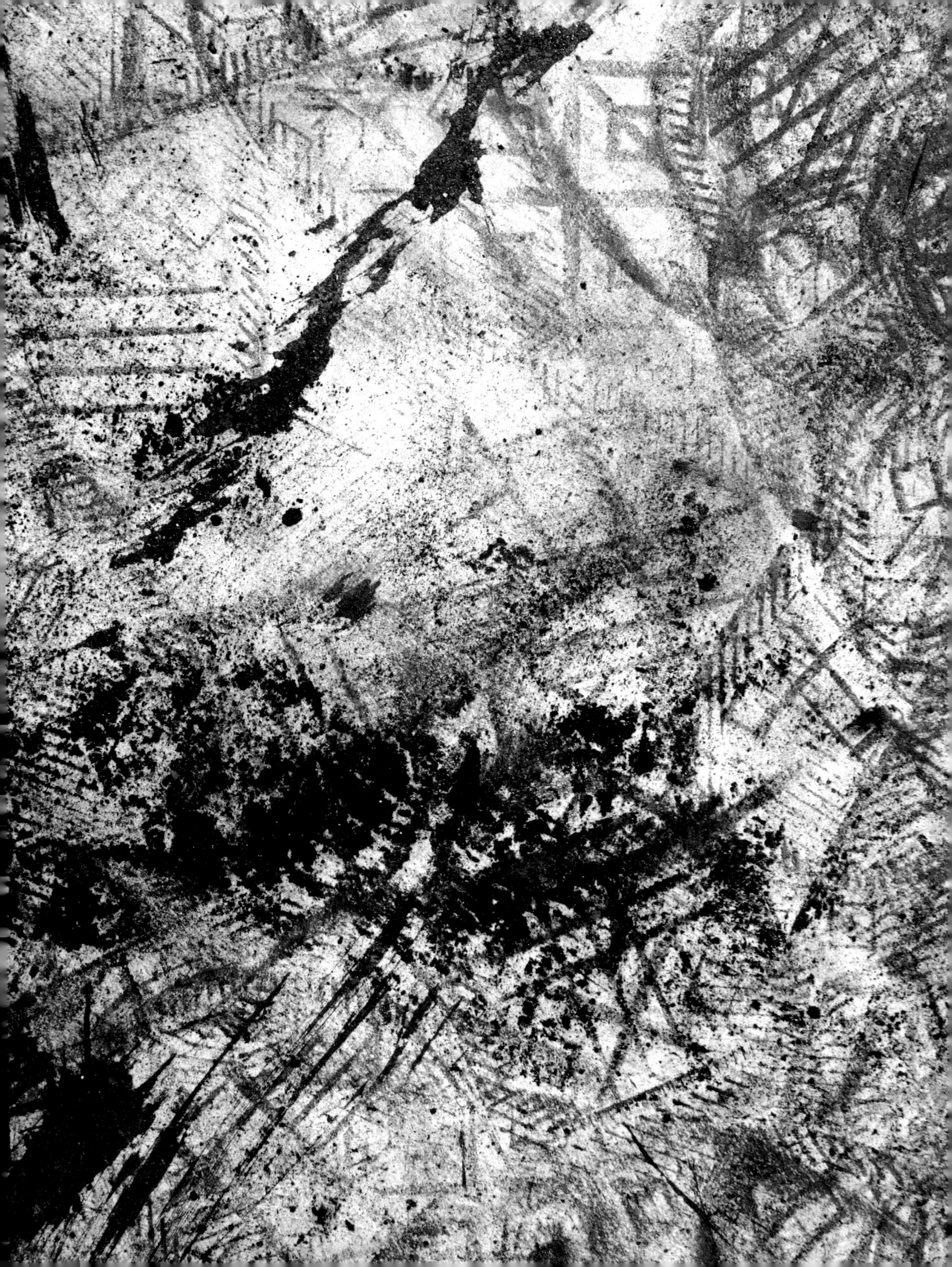

FOREWORD

Tony Lewis: Anthology 2014–2016 is the first in a new series of books that spotlights significant acquisitions by the Hirshhorn Museum and Sculpture Garden and offer fresh scholarship on artists' practice and work. Although new acquisitions to the Museum are often given pride of place in our galleries or Garden, it has become clear that new publications featuring focused and groundbreaking research allow for deeper understandings of both the artworks themselves—often radical and boundary-pushing—and the ways in which they enhance and broaden our collection.

Tony Lewis is an apt figure to launch this new series: highly experimental and introspective, and dedicated to the intricacies of his chosen media—graphite and paper—he is at the forefront of a generation of young African American artists who are moving forward the possibilities of abstraction as it develops in the twenty-first century. In 2018, the Hirshhorn acquired and exhibited his titular suite of thirty-four collage-poems, each compellingly focused on remaking and reenvisioning a touchstone of American childhood culture: the comic strip *Calvin and Hobbes*. Redrawing, obscuring, refashioning, and transforming this staple of the comics page, Lewis comes up with palimpsests both mysterious and powerful, poetry drawn from the highly physical way in which he interacts with his preferred materials. Ranging from the gnomic (*glik glik glik*) to the allusive (*The She; Life Doubt*) to the ominous (*Slaughterhouse; The Monsters Monsters*), the artworks he fashions out of the raw material of comic strips are collages of individual drawings that explore the collaborative nature of creativity and authorship, leaving meaning open to a range of interpretations.

Lewis's work extends, of course, beyond *Anthology*, and this catalogue highlights many of the ways in

Tony Lewis's studio floor, 2022

which the artist is working to collapse the boundaries between seemingly disparate art forms. Lewis has quickly established himself in the contemporary art world by forming a distinct visual vocabulary that integrates poetry and text with the properties of abstraction, and his monochromatic drawings pull from various visual and written sources, ranging from the personal to the political. Separating, rearranging, and erasing text, he shifts the way we move through language to open up new and unexpected readings.

Lewis grapples with his materials in a manner many have described as deeply athletic. Profoundly attuned to the ways in which paper and graphite interact, blur, wear away, and obscure each other, he combines the cerebral concerns of abstract art with a physical, almost Romantic engagement with material in a way that advances abstraction in highly idiosyncratic directions. At the same time, his practice engages questions of representation and language, challenging the viewer while hovering just out of reach of rational comprehension. As such, his work is a nonpareil addition to the Hirshhorn collection, and this investigation of its methods and aims serves as a thought-provoking launch pad for our new series of books on our most compelling acquisitions—which are, like the Hirshhorn itself, evocative, radical, and forever moving beyond the expected.

We thank the contributors to this catalogue, including the artists Theaster Gates and Karl Haendel, for their insights into Lewis's practice and oeuvre. We also offer our gratitude to Theaster Gates for his generous support of the publication. We also thank Betsy Johnson, assistant curator, and Laura Harger, senior editor, for overseeing the catalogue's production. Most of all, we thank Tony Lewis himself for sharing his words and works with our public.

Melissa Chiu

Director, Hirshhorn Museum and Sculpture Garden

ACKNOWLEDGMENTS

The acquisition of this remarkable body of work by the Hirshhorn, as well as its exhibition at the Museum in 2018, would not have been possible without the enthusiastic support of many devoted individuals. First and foremost, my deepest thanks and sincere admiration go to the artist, whose willingness to plumb the depths of his experience resonates throughout his powerful work. I thank him for his generosity of spirit, intellectual stamina, and wholehearted eagerness to engage with every step of the process. Chenée Lewis, at the Tony Lewis Studio, has been a constant source of light and positivity, and I am grateful for the personal care that she took with this project. The Hirshhorn also extends its profound thanks to Theaster Gates for his generous support of this book.

Flavio del Monte, of MASSIMODECARLO, provided exceptional support in the realization of this project, and I offer my sincere thanks to him for being such a good-natured, enjoyable companion on this journey. Shane and Julie Campbell, of Shane Campbell Gallery, also provided support for the exhibition and were among the first to recognize and nurture this talented artist, for which we are eternally grateful.

For handling the installation of this nuanced work at the Hirshhorn in 2018 with elegance and sensitivity, I thank my exceptional colleagues. I extend special thanks to director Melissa Chiu; former deputy director Elizabeth Duggal; and former chief curator Stéphane Aquin for their dedicated support of this project, ensuring that it found a space and a home within the Hirshhorn. And for their guidance and encouragement, I thank the rest of my curatorial colleagues: head curator Evelyn C. Hankins; former curator Mark Beasley; former associate curator Mika Yoshitake; associate curator Anne Reeve;

Tony Lewis (b. Los Angeles, California, 1986), *Untitled (Orange)*, 2021 (detail). Colored pencil, graphite powder, and rubber cement on paper; $41\frac{9}{16}$ × 27 in. (105.6 × 68.6 cm) associate curator Marina Isgro; former assistant curator Sandy Guttman; curatorial assistant Alice Phan; and especially curator-at-large Gianni Jetzer, who first spotted Lewis's work and eagerly brought it to our attention.

Robust appreciation goes to supervisory exhibits specialists Scott Larson and Larissa Raddell; former manager of exhibitions and curatorial planning Lawrence Hyman; director of exhibitions, design, and special projects Al Masino; former exhibition designer John Klink; lighting designer Austin Shull; former director of collections Sarah Stauderman; former chief registrar Rajshree Solanki; head registrar Andrea Jain; conservators Stephanie Lussier and Briana Feston-Brunet; former editor Amy Pastan and associate editor Deane Madsen; designer Beth Skirkanich; director of public engagement Kevin Hull; public engagement manager Amy Bahr; former director of communications and marketing Allison Peck; former communications associate and public affairs coordinator Madeline Feller; digital asset manager Julia Murphy; former social media manager Hilary-Morgan Watt; former director of advancement Emily Moqtaderi; former advancement associate Heidi Sweely; former director of administration and finance Chris Wailoo; current director of administration and finance Judy Brown; and photographer Alex Jamison.

A small publication such as this one still encounters many challenges, and I am grateful to senior editor Laura Harger for being a steadfast partner in steering this project through choppy water. Contributors Theaster Gates and Karl Haendel offer glimpses into Lewis's work that are simultaneously personal and universal, which is no easy feat, and I thank them for going the extra distance to help others connect to the work. Head of publications Ilaria Bombelli and designer Marcello Jacopo Biffi at Mousse Publishing were an absolute joy to work with, and I appreciate the energy and passion that they brought to the design of this book. Published four years after the exhibition of the work, this book has been buoyed by the hard work of many new Hirshhorn colleagues, including deputy director Jaya Kaveeshwar; exhibition and curatorial planning manager Liza Strelka; and director of communications and marketing Kate Gibbs. I thank them for their dedicated support of this artist and his vision.

Last, my deepest gratitude goes to my parents, Linda Wallace and Kenneth Johnson, who orchestrated a childhood full of opportunities to connect to art and encouraged me to find my own voice, and to my grandparents Donna and Wayne Johnson, who taught me the importance of books.

Betsy Johnson

Assistant Curator, Hirshhorn Museum and Sculpture Garden

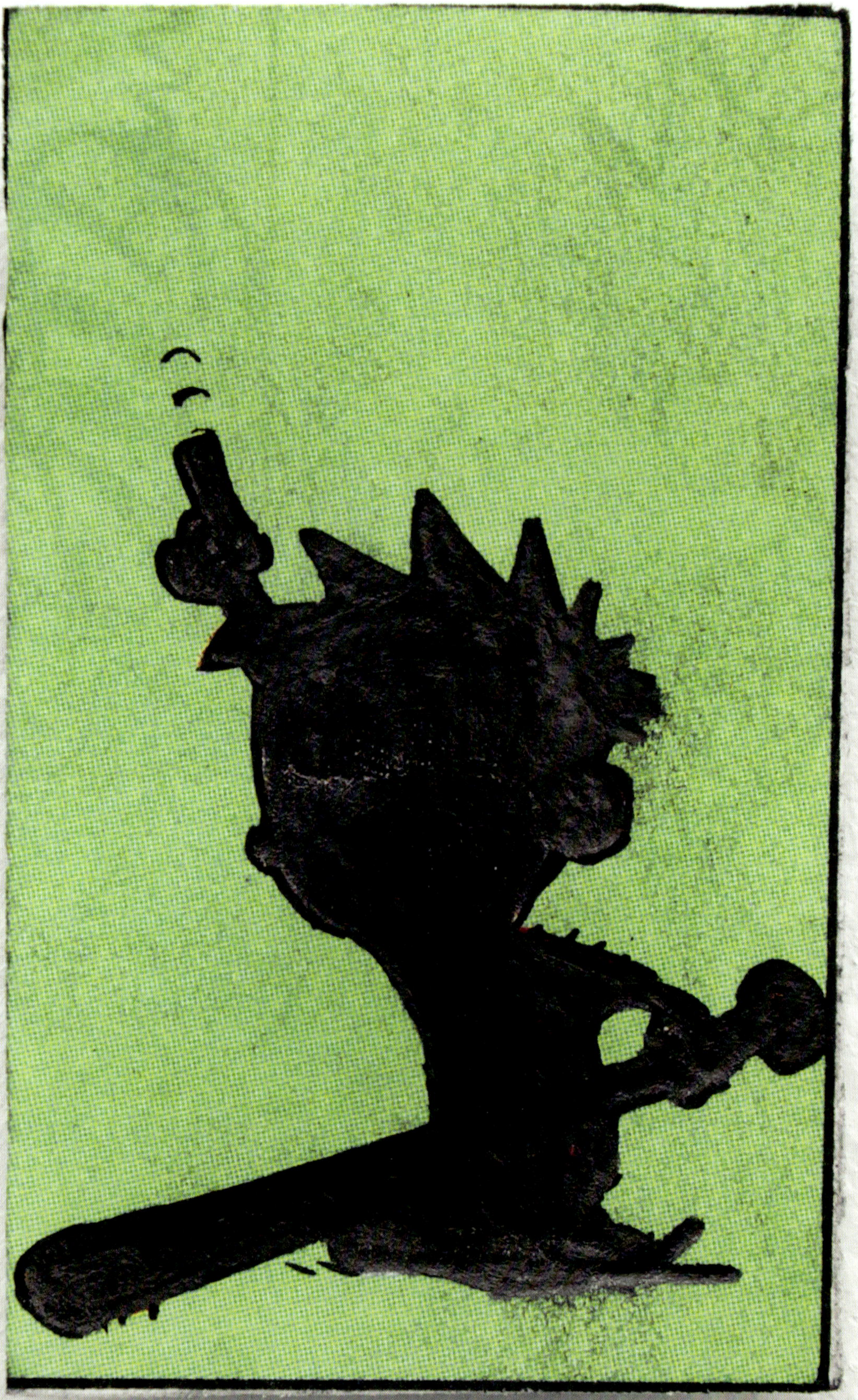

RUMBLING INTO A VOLCANO
THE NATURE OF SURFACE IN THE ART OF TONY LEWIS

Betsy Johnson

In 2013, Chicago-based artist Tony Lewis sat down with a comic book that he had cherished since childhood and began to disassemble it. Folding and ripping, he separated out each frame, setting them free from the narrative like so many pearls cut loose from the thread stringing them together. He then began to carve out more space within them, layering graphite and correction tape in thick swaths over text and image alike until only a handful of words floating in cavernous speech bubbles remained. Later, as he sat surrounded by piles of these small drawings (fig. 2), he began to see the tenor of the language shift and change as he rearranged the frames, giving them new life in poems that expanded the world of his source material, Bill Watterson's comic strip *Calvin and Hobbes.*

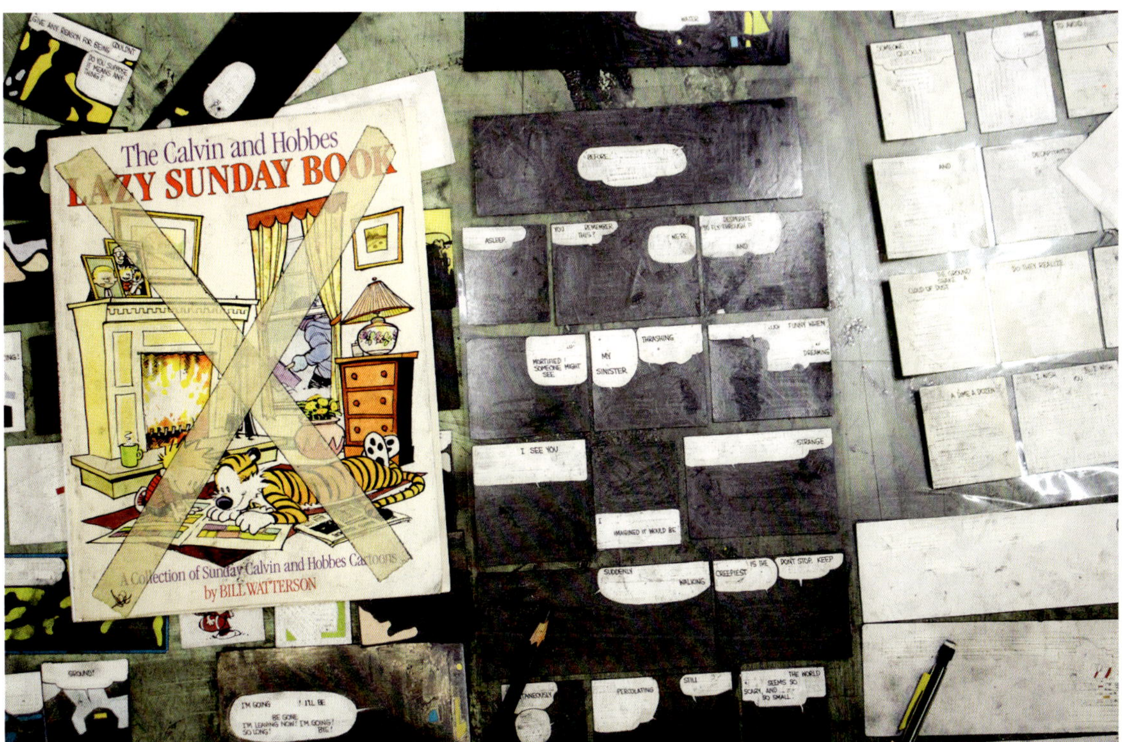

Fig. 2. Individual comic frames laid out on Tony Lewis's studio floor, 2022

Fig. 1. Tony Lewis, *Untitled*, 2013. Pencil, graphite powder, and correction fluid on comic-book cutout; $2\frac{1}{8} \times 1\frac{3}{8}$ in. (5.4 × 3.5 cm)

Many stories begin to explain how Lewis arrived at this point. First, there is a boy who is presented with a copy of *The Authoritative Calvin and Hobbes* (1990) by his father as a reward for a high score on an exam. Inside this treasure, he discovers sketches that open a window onto new ways of being, catapulting his imagination to heights of absurdity and depths of profundity. Years later, as he moves into a small art studio, his first after graduate school, he brings this book with him, and one day he opens it and begins to cut, fold, and tear out the frames—an act simultaneously so terrifying and so exhilarating that he knows he must keep going (fig. 3).

There are added layers of nuance to this tale. There is the boy who is inspired to draw after falling in love with the world of *Calvin and Hobbes*, a comic in which a young Black boy like himself never appeared. And, years later, that boy becomes a man who, after tearing apart this cherished book, starts to draw a lush, beautiful afro over Calvin's spiky hair (p. 32). Then there is the college athlete who sustains an injury during his sophomore year that leaves him permanently on the sidelines. In art, he finds a way to remain rooted in the physical world, integrating his mind and body through the manipulation of materials.

One more story covers each frame with a dusting of dark, glistening graphite—similar to that which spreads across the floor of Lewis's graduate school studio, landing there first as an accident and then as an intention. Coating the walls and seeping under the door into the hallways and neighboring spaces, the graphite becomes a living, breathing force hitching a ride on feet, hands, and air (fig. 4). Eventually it catches the attention of authorities, who sound alarms in the name of health and safety and the common good and issue an order to clean the studio, chasing the dark material into captivity. And the artist finds himself back where he started, in a gleaming studio that reveals traces of the practices of others but none of his own.

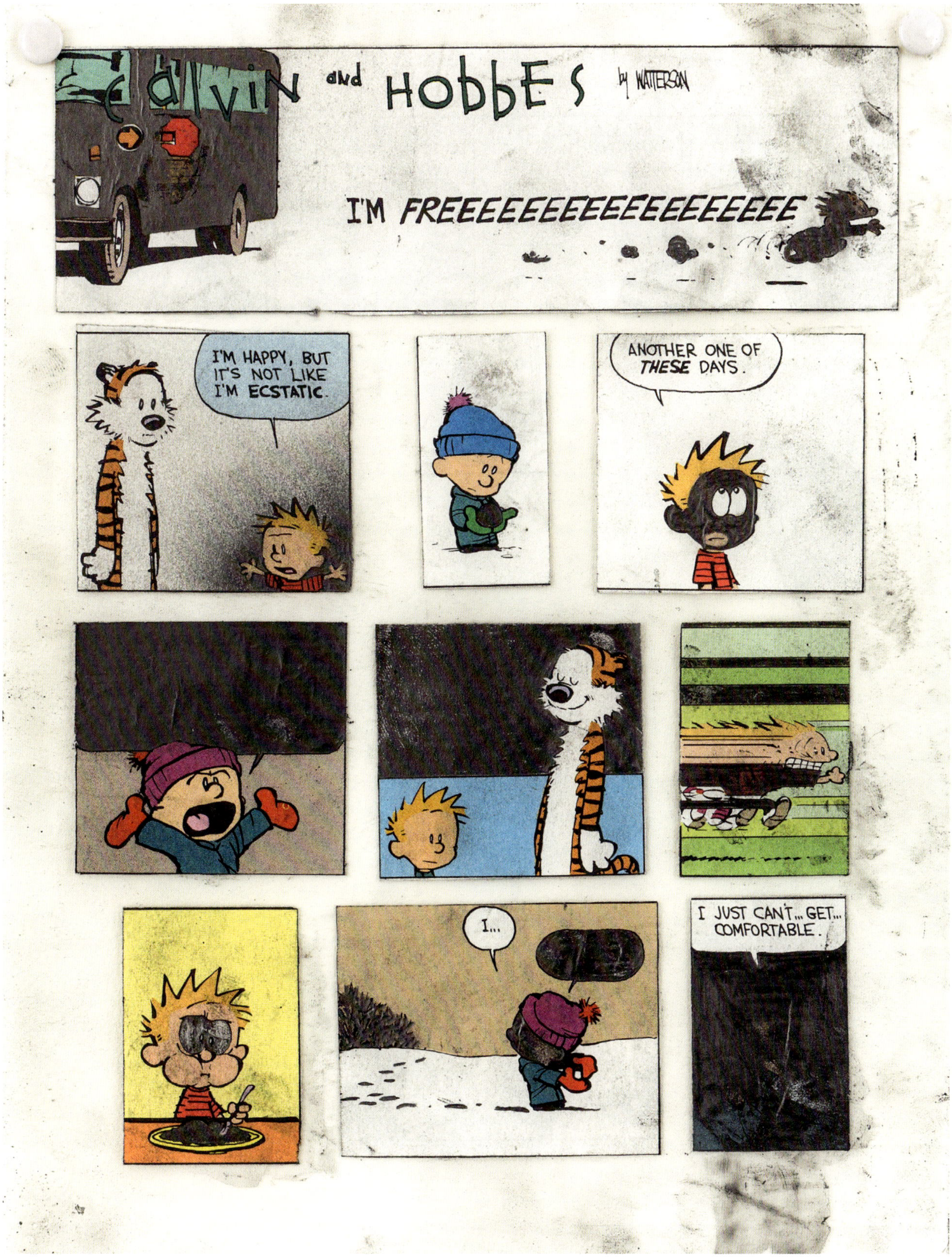

Fig. 3. Tony Lewis, *Another One of These Days*, 2014. Pencil and graphite powder on paper and transparency; 11 × 8½ in. (27.9 × 21.6 cm)

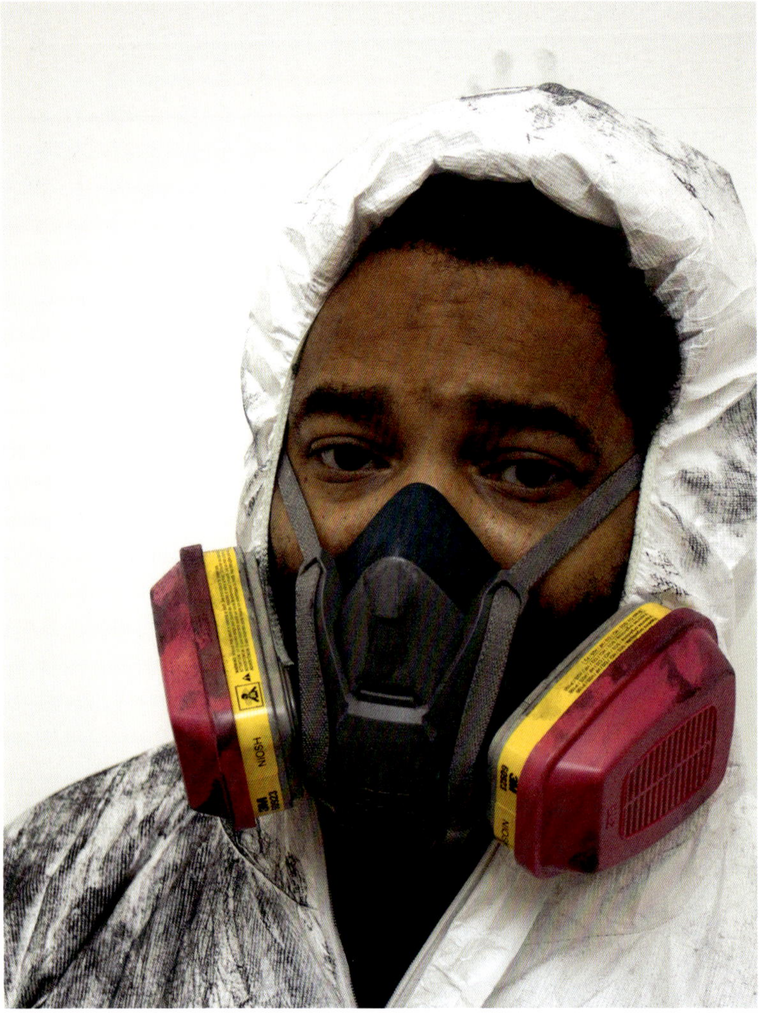

Fig. 4. Tony Lewis in the studio, 2022

Lewis's collage-poems are born equally from these moments: a boy in awe of the power of the medium, an athlete reveling in the physicality of art-making, an artist mourning the loss of his first truly fertile space, and a man reclaiming the stories he has been told. There are other stories, of course—they pile up, one on top of another, until there is a sea of them, just as the frames of *Calvin and Hobbes* spilled out of the book and across Lewis's floor. Each story contains fragments from which the future is built.

The way Lewis tells it, he was never a confident creative writer until he began to write through drawing. To explain it another way, he designed a system through which to write poems that began by turning language into a physical thing that he could wrestle with, push against, and manipulate using the tools he had committed himself to: his favorite 9B Caran d'Ache graphite stick, plenty of loose graphite powder, adhesives, and correction tape. And he took it one step further: he created a framework for making poems that echoes that of the Sunday comic, with a long title frame at the top followed by three rows of shorter frames, sometimes punctuated by a circle (see fig. 3). Once Lewis had this structure in place, words began to play off one another, allowing relationships and meanings to rise into visibility. It was as if the drawings had become collaborators in the writing of poetry; as if the poems came into being almost of their own accord. By the end of 2016, Lewis had completed a series of thirty-four collages composed of 322 drawings that he titled *Anthology 2014–2016*.

When I think of the method that Lewis employed to write, I am reminded of Tristan Tzara's instructions on how to write a Dadaist poem:

To make a dadaist poem
Take a newspaper.
Take a pair of scissors.
Choose an article as long as you are planning
to make your poem.
Cut out the article.
Then cut out each of the words that make up
this article and put them in a bag.
Shake it gently.
Then take out the scraps one after the other
in the order in which they left the bag.
Copy conscientiously.
The poem will be like you.
And here you are a writer, infinitely original and
endowed with a sensibility that is charming though
beyond the understanding of the vulgar.[1]

Originating in Zürich during the tumultuous period of the First World War, Dada was a celebration of nonsense and irrationality as devices to liberate humanity from the logic-driven forces that had led to violent conflict. *Dada* itself was a meaningless moniker, accidentally "found" in a dictionary and immediately recognized by all as expressing the spirit of the movement in the way it trips off the tongue. Taken up by poets, writers, and artists, Dada's irreverence strongly influenced the development of twentieth-century art, opening up new avenues of exploration in the formerly uncharted territories of the unconscious, the abject, and the unknown. Whereas Tzara's instructions for poetry promoted the element of chance to access these regions, other Dadaist artists, such as Hugo Ball, experimented with onomatopoeia in sound poetry, wielding syllables as if they were musical notes to build poems that function without legible words (fig. 5).

KARAWANE

jolifanto bambla ô falli bambla
grossiga m'pfa habla horem
égiga goramen
higo bloiko russula huju
hollaka hollala
anlogo bung
blago bung
blago bung
bosso fataka
ü üü ü
schampa wulla wussa ólobo
hej tatta gôrem
eschige zunbada
wulubu ssubudu uluw ssubudu
tumba ba- umf
kusagauma
ba - umf

(1917)
Hugo Ball
53

Fig. 5. Hugo Ball (b. Pirmasens, Germany, 1886–1927), *Karawane*, 1917, as published in the 1920 *Dada Almanach*

These early experiments served as a springboard for later movements such as Surrealism, Fluxus, Conceptual art, and concrete and visual poetry, fostering an ethos that became a fertile ground for the development of Lewis's art.

Lewis's practice contains reverberations of these forerunners who challenged the limits of what art is and how it is made. Like Tzara, Lewis invents formulas for his creative process, explaining that for him, "the purpose of the studio is to find new ways to make drawings."[2] As a result, his practice is composed of multiple bodies of work that are simultaneously distinct and overlapping, with each series obeying an internal logic that he has set in place through guidelines that dictate its scale, materials, and composition. Within this framework, each body of work represents "one viable way to make a drawing."[3] Once a new type of drawing is established, it becomes part of Lewis's overarching practice, meaning that his series are very rarely brought to a definitive end, instead intermingling at exhibitions like a rotating cast of characters in a play.

One might understand Lewis's process of honing a consistent framework that is repeatedly and intuitively applied to generate new works as a systemic practice that participates in the Conceptual legacy of art-making summed up by Sol LeWitt's oft-repeated phrase "The idea becomes a machine that makes the art." At the time he wrote his seminal essay "Paragraphs on Conceptual Art" in 1967, LeWitt was both an artist heavily invested in New York's emergent Conceptual art movement and one of the first writers to attempt to put its guiding principles into words.[4] It is useful to understand Lewis's practice against the backdrop of LeWitt's longer statement:

When an artist uses a conceptual form of art, it means that all of the planning and decisions are made beforehand and the execution is a perfunctory affair. The idea becomes a machine that makes the art. This kind of art is not theoretical or illustrative of theories; it is intuitive, it is involved with all types of mental processes and it is purposeless.[5]

Where Lewis's practice diverges from the models provided by Dada and Conceptual art is in its unwillingness to relinquish physical labor, composition, and personal expression. Unlike the Dadaist surrender to chance or the allegiance of the Conceptual artist to the idea, which LeWitt describes as fully formed and unchangeable once art-making has commenced, Lewis is strongly motivated by a desire to physically interact with the material, and he holds fast to his right to make compositional decisions throughout the entire process of creating. The framework for each "viable way to make a drawing" then functions as a site within which a multitude of choices are encountered and decisions made. Lewis explains:

I wasn't specifically thinking of Dada when making this work; I was ironically thinking of coherent writing, starting from an incoherent place—it was more like a puzzle or a word game: when the small drawings/non-sense phrases click into place grammatically or in terms of linguistic meaning, do I follow that path or not? Sometimes I did, and sometimes I didn't. It was more rhythm-based and less reactive.[6]

Interestingly, Lewis has remarked that it was the initial creation of the drawings from the comic that were, in his mind, "more related to Dada, in that it was a reaction to [an] author—a way to go from sense to nonsense. The making of collage and the poem was a way to bring it back to sense and original thought writing."[7] Thus, in order to find his own voice in the language of *Calvin and Hobbes*, Lewis created chaos and then reestablished order.

Rhythm is an organizing factor that Lewis employs as a means of bringing order to chaos. If we consider his process through the lens of music, instead of assembling sound samples in chance configurations in the manner of John Cage, Lewis interacts with his found material like a jazz musician, improvising with the samples until they reach new, unexpected, and, most importantly, endless possibilities. There is a cadence in the spacing of Lewis's *Anthology* collage-poems, with heavy pauses in the journey countered at times by a surprise tumbling of words stacked one on top of another. Let us consider, for instance, the first poem of the series, *Surface* (fig. 6), composed of nine drawings laid out in four rows. Following the convention of Sunday comics, the top frame is wide and narrow, spanning the entire row, with the text it contains announcing the title of the piece. Although one might expect a certain boldness in the title frame, the word "Surface" appears at the bottom of the speech bubble, its letters smudged and muted by a dark cloud of graphite that adheres to the correction tape, which is perfectly sized to blanket the rows of text above it. There is a soft, pensive quality hanging in this frame, almost as if the word is spoken in a whisper.

As we read through the rest of the frames, the placement of the words—their proximity, position, and legibility—influences how they enter our field of vision and our mind. "Look" jumps out brightly from the top left of the second row, followed by a deep pause before we run into "hard" as if into a wall and then fall downward through the next four frames ("what" / "putrid" / "heavy steaming" / "thing."), landing on the last with the weight of gravity emphasized by the finality of a period. We rise again in the next two frames, musing "how mysterious and" / "brave" before crashing back down to the finale: "rumbling into a volcano." This is not text pulled from a bag—it is a composition of highs and lows, expansion and collapse, where meaning is formed equally by the language and the space around it.

This spatial relationship to language has deep roots in Conceptual art, and it is no surprise that it was

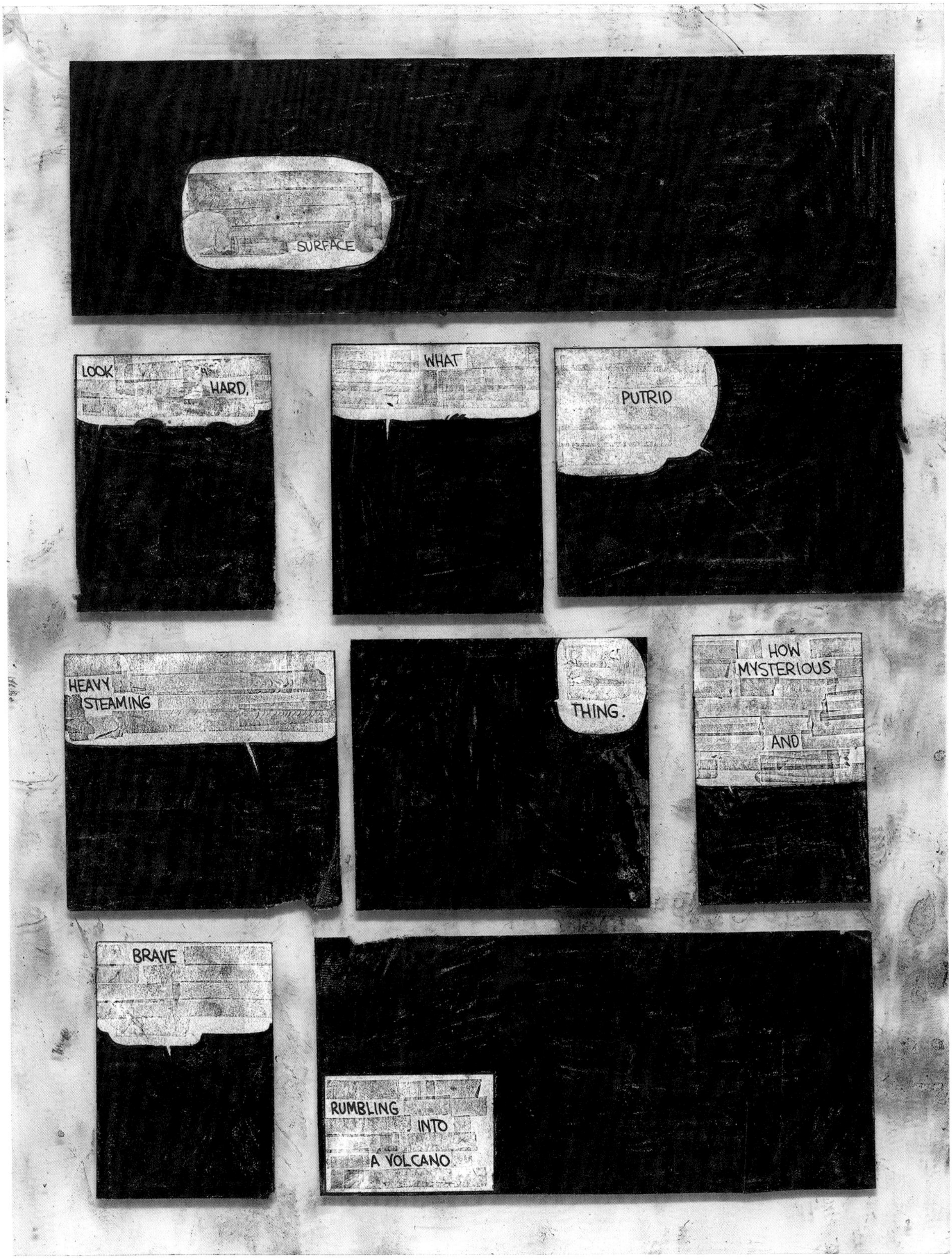

Fig. 6. Tony Lewis, *Surface*, 2014, from *Anthology 2014–2016*, 2014–2016. Graphite, correction tape, and paper collage (comics) on transparency; 11 × 8½ in. (27.9 × 21.6 cm). Joseph H. Hirshhorn Purchase Fund, 2019 (2019.012.01)

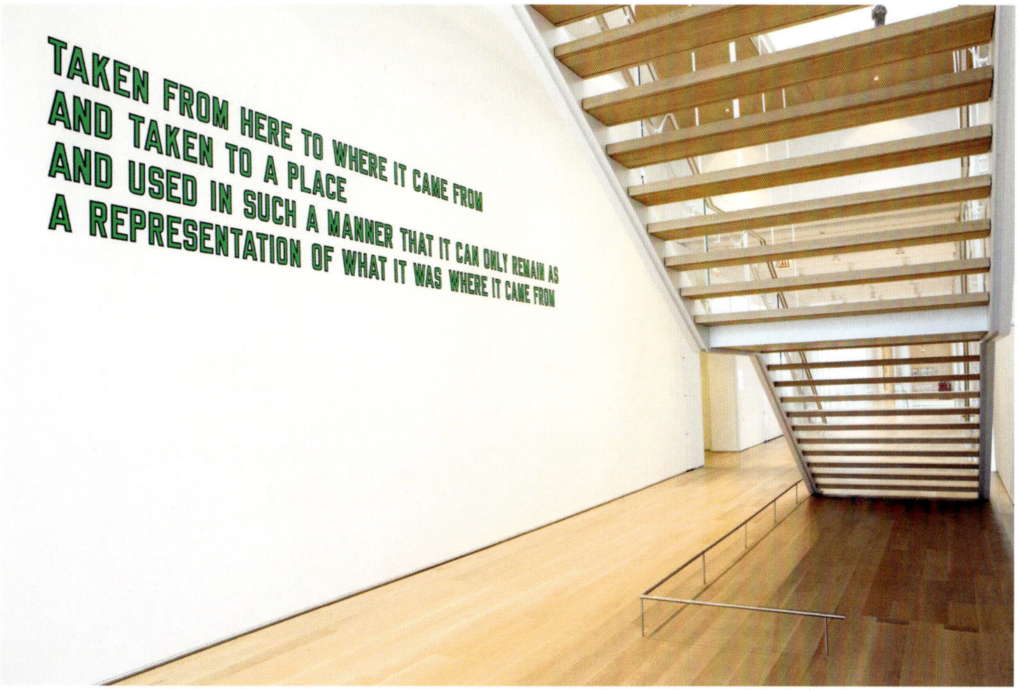

Fig. 7. Lawrence Weiner (b. Bronx, New York, 1941–2021), *TAKEN FROM HERE TO WHERE IT CAME FROM AND TAKEN TO A PLACE AND USED IN SUCH A MANNER THAT IT CAN ONLY REMAIN AS A REPRESENTATION OF WHAT IT WAS WHERE IT CAME FROM*, 1980. Dimensions variable. Gift of Coosje van Bruggen and Claes Oldenburg. The Art Institute of Chicago (1982.402)

through the work of Conceptual art pioneer Lawrence Weiner that Lewis came to the idea of using language as a material in the first place. There is a work by Weiner (fig. 7) installed in a hallway at the Art Institute of Chicago that Lewis first saw around 2010 and returned to again and again to read its thick green stenciled letters stretching out along the wall:

TAKEN FROM HERE TO WHERE IT CAME FROM
AND TAKEN TO A PLACE
AND USED IN SUCH A MANNER THAT IT CAN
ONLY REMAIN AS
A REPRESENTATION OF WHAT IT WAS WHERE
IT CAME FROM

At first, this work infuriated Lewis because he felt it should, as a piece of writing, contain a direct, discernable message. Instead, there is a level of ambiguity to the text that leaves its legibility flickering just out of reach. Lewis explains, "I just didn't understand what it was saying, why it was art, and why it was so high on the wall. I found it to be poetic and a fleeting statement with great grammatical rhythm, but I was lost every time I put concrete thought to it."[8] It took a while for Lewis to understand Weiner's assertion that language can be sculpture. That one can build objects with letters as one might use graphite, paint, stone, or any other material to represent something beyond itself, outside its normal function, and larger than the sum of its parts. Language can be deconstructed, excavated, and reconfigured in a way that creates space for new meanings to flourish in the hazy, fertile ground of the mind.

From the start, Lewis's experimentations with language have explored the endless possibilities inherent in a single text through erasure and a playful redirection of pathways of reading. In an early text-based series begun in 2010, *Untitled (People of color peopled color, and the color of people colored people.)*, Lewis created a template by positioning the text (which also serves as the series title) across a seven-by-five-foot expanse of paper. Each drawing in the series contains an excerpt of the original text—letters, words, and phrases that assume their correct position on the page when they appear. Sometimes the excerpted text is legible on its own; other times, it is not. Each work is finished with a single hand-drawn line that wraps around and cuts through the fragmentary words, binding them together and inviting the reader to deviate from the standard pathway—left to right, top to bottom—to interact with the text in unusual, and often incoherent, ways.

Perhaps the easiest way to understand what Lewis was doing with this first series is to closely examine one of the works (fig. 8). Elements have been extracted from the original text so that only three full words ("People of color") and parts of two others ("and" and "of") remain on the page. The line drawn over this text begins at the upper left edge of the paper, slicing through "People" and then cutting back down and across through the letters "a" and "d." It then slopes up to the far right of the first row and works its way backward through "of color" before plummeting abruptly downward through "o." The work is straightforwardly titled according to this alternate reading of the text: *People ad roloc foo*. What Lewis has done here is to create space for new pathways within the structure to which language is normally bound—that which is dictated by its purpose as a vehicle for meaning. In vacating this singular purpose, Lewis opens up other modes of reading and, in so doing, manages to question and perhaps even dispel some of language's authoritative power. What happens to "color" when we read it backward? It becomes "roloc," an incoherent string of letters, divested of symbolic meaning and reduced to sound and form. And in this humble state, set free from the chains of meaning, writing becomes something else—it becomes "one viable way to make a drawing." By challenging the assumption that language must be encountered in a predetermined manner, Lewis has created room for play.

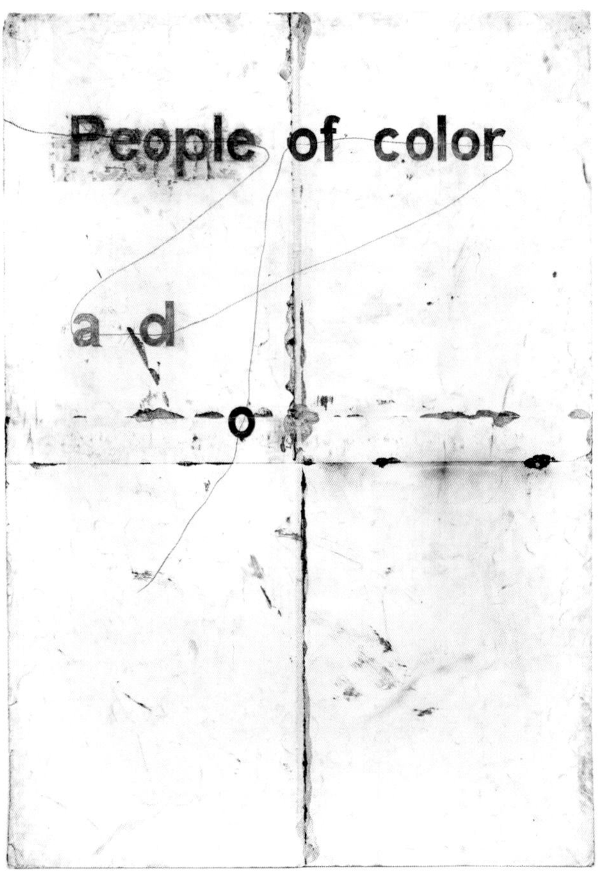

Fig. 8. Tony Lewis, *People ad roloc foo*, 2012. Pencil and graphite powder on paper; 84 × 60 in. (213.4 × 152.4 cm)

Two elements came together in this early body of work that remain integral to this day. First, Lewis utilizes language toward which he feels a certain amount of curiosity and/or ambivalence. He has always engaged in the act of writing, filling notebooks with words and phrases that sometimes come together in ways that challenge him to engage with them more deeply. This was the case with the sentence that runs beneath the *Untitled (People of color. . .)* series—a statement of Lewis's own creation that he wanted to sit with and contemplate for a while. Sometimes, however, he has sought an external voice to consider alongside his own. Later series appropriated aphorisms from H. Jackson Brown Jr.'s *Life's Little Instruction Book* (1991; fig. 9),[9] instructions from Alma Chestnut Moore's *How to Clean Everything* (1961), speech bubble text from *Calvin and Hobbes*, and, in more recent work, the losing rebuttal made by William F. Buckley Jr. in his legendary 1965 debate with James Baldwin at the University of Cambridge. Running throughout all these source texts is a voice that Lewis pushes against (even when it is his own), sometimes accepting the wisdom offered and at other times rejecting it, recognizing when it does and does not speak to his own lived experience.

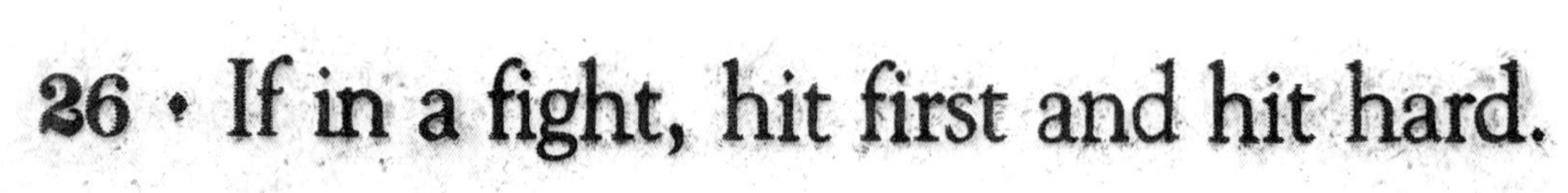

Fig. 9. Tony Lewis, *26 • If in a fight, hit first and hit hard*, 2016. Pencil, graphite powder, screws, and rubber bands; dimensions variable. Installation view, *The Revolution Will Not Be Gray*, Aspen Art Museum, Colorado, 2016

The second element that is critical to Lewis's practice is that the physical life of the object is written into its very surface. In the *Untitled (People of color . . .)* series, each seven-by-five-foot drawing is composed of four smaller sheets of paper that Lewis laid on the floor and joined together with tape and rubber cement. In doing so, he made no efforts to conceal the joining of the sheets; nor did he attempt to keep them a pristine white. Quite the opposite—to avoid facing the white page, Lewis chooses to build upon paper already scuffed, creased, torn, and smudged. He prefers to work upon a ground that shows its history instead of one that pretends to have none. Challenging the association of whiteness with purity, cleanliness, and desirability, he finds beauty and interest in what others might characterize as dirty, messy, unshapely, or abject.

Lewis is not alone in using language that travels in and out of legibility to expose how words are wielded, comprehended, boxed in, or broken out: Glenn Ligon is a contemporary who has created works that call attention to the additional meanings that arise when language is pushed into abstraction. Ligon's seminal text-based work *Untitled (Four Etchings)* (1992; fig. 10) appropriates text from Zora Neale Hurston's "How It Feels to Be Colored Me" (1928) to illustrate how the common use of black type on white paper replicates the conspicuousness of Blackness and the experience of otherness in a world dominated by white privilege. In Ligon's work, the ink blurs and obfuscates the language toward the bottom of the page as the text is printed again and again, the splotches of illegibility staging a rebellion against forms of knowing that are predicated on stark tonal difference. Likewise, Lewis chooses to work upon surfaces that have already been enriched by contact with graphite via hands, feet, and air as a means of unsettling the primacy of linguistic meaning and opening up layers of nuance that arise when words are freed of their allegiance to syntax and become one more compositional element in a drawing.

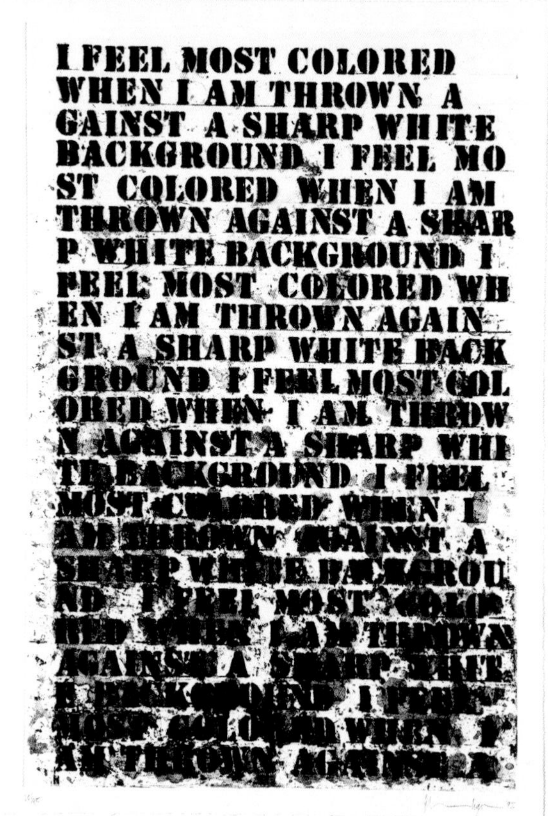

Fig. 10. Glenn Ligon (b. Bronx, New York, 1960), *Untitled (Four Etchings)* (detail), 1992. Suite of 4; softground etching, aquatint, spit bite, and sugarlift on paper; 25 × 17⅜ in. (63.5 × 44.2 cm) each. Edition of 45 and 10 APs. Joseph H. Hirshhorn Purchase Fund, 1993 (93.4.2)

Lewis's interest in surfaces that register their use can be best understood through an ongoing body of work: the floor drawings (fig. 11). These works are an homage to his first studio, the one that was undone when the graphite layering its surfaces was deemed dirty and potentially hazardous and was forcibly cleaned. Creating his first floor drawing in 2011, Lewis laboriously rubbed graphite into paper that spanned the entire floor of a friend's gallery, essentially turning its surface into a drawing that visitors added to as they walked across it. At the end of the exhibition, the drawing was pulled up and sent to another exhibition, and another, and another—each time taking on a new life in a changed state, growing more sculptural as it became torn, creased, and fragmented in its travels. In the past decade, Lewis has made ten floor drawings that have traveled to close to forty exhibitions, continually evolving and charting a life course of their own.

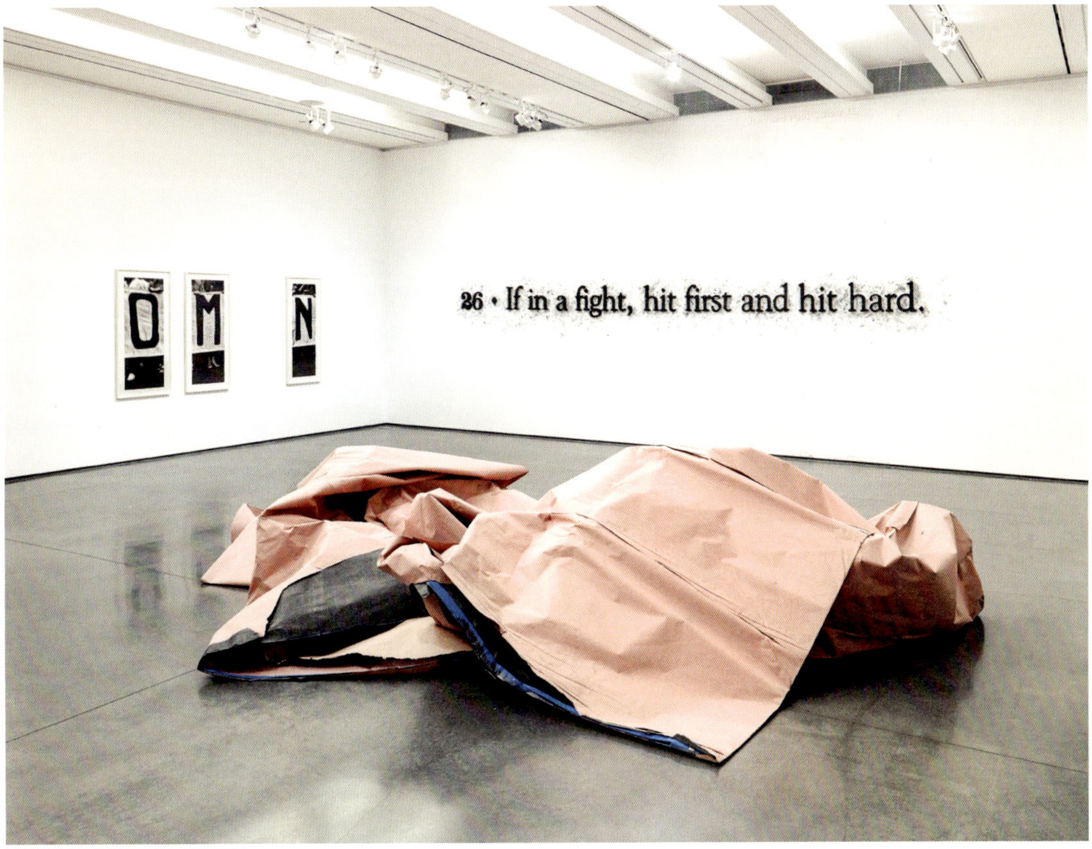

Fig. 11. Tony Lewis, floor drawing, 2016. Graphite powder, paint, and tape on paper; dimensions variable. Installation view, *The Revolution Will Not Be Gray*, Aspen Art Museum, Colorado, 2016

What becomes evident in these architecturally scaled floor drawings, and which also holds true for the intimate works in *Anthology 2014–2016*, is the critical role that graphite plays in Lewis's practice. It is graphite's unruly nature, leaving traces on fingers and surfaces and even intermingling with the very air that Lewis breathes, that gives it the capacity to infuse his works with vitality. Although the uncontrollable nature of this medium often earns it comparisons with dirt and detritus, Lewis has described the use of graphite in his floor drawings as a means of purifying the space. This is how he leads us to see this material: as a significant collaborator in his creative process, providing the ground upon which all is constructed, recording the passage of time, and keeping the work alive through its changeability. This is a reframing of the nature of the surface that one makes a drawing upon—obfuscating the white page under a layer of graphite that attests to use, to handling, and even to time in the way that nothing ever remains untouched.

In Lewis's work, the handling of the object, no matter its scale, is a language in and of itself. In the *Anthology 2014–2016* series, there is a communication in the act of cutting up a treasured manuscript, holding each frame as an object, and pressing it between one's fingers—a missive recorded in the smudges of fingerprints. Lewis is processing language through his body, trying to come to an understanding of what it means to him by physically handling and manipulating it. Sometimes the correction tape and the graphite begin to obliterate the remaining words, causing their messages to seem like they might flicker out of existence at any moment, leaving some marks so faint as to be nearly unrecognizable, confused with and by the accretions that join them on the page. At other times, the graphite gathers along the edge of a line of tape, seemingly bent on forming its own language.

For Lewis, each step of this process—the disassembly of the book, the creation of the individual drawings, the compilation of the collage-poems, and, last but not least, the publication of those poems in a book—unfolded in a chain of events that were separate yet connected, each leading naturally and undeniably to the next. For him, the end result is the poetry. Poetry that he has described as "the clearest form of writing" he has ever done:

> It's deeply personal work, and I think because of where it came from and because of what happens with the collages, it ends up being something that it's almost hard to talk about because it's probably some of the most vulnerable, some of the most personal work . . . because the making of it exists outside of the studio where the rest of the work is made. Outside of the context of where the other drawings are made. This is made at a desk, and because of the process of the collages, for me it ends up being probably the clearest form of writing I've ever done.[10]

He knows that the audience of his work might feel differently—some might prefer to linger in the dense materiality of the collages, feeling the texture of the materials, their weight pressed into the paper. But for Lewis, it was important to set the language free.

Let us return to *Surface*. For me, this poem says everything.

Surface

Look hard, what putrid
Heavy
    Steaming thing. How
Mysterious
And
Brave
Rumbling
                    Into
A Volcano

1. Tristan Tzara, "Dada Manifesto 1918," *Dada 3* (December 1918); repr. in Robert Motherwell, ed., *The Dada Painters and Poets: An Anthology* (Cambridge, MA: Belknap Press of Harvard University Press, 1951), 92.
2. Tony Lewis quoted in Josh Usmani, "Tony Lewis to Discuss 'Action and Language' in Art at MOCA Exhibition Talk," *Cleveland Scene*, June 3, 2015, www.clevescene.com/cleveland/tony-lewis-to-discuss-action-and-language-in-art-at-moca-exhibition-talk/.
3. See Lewis's description of his *Untitled (People of color peopled color, and the color of people colored people.)* project, begun in 2010: "There is variation at each stage of mark-making, but I've ultimately come to understand the project as one viable way to make a drawing." In Kevin Blake, "Drawing Lines of Communication: A Conversation with Tony Lewis," *Bad at Sports* (blog), April 2, 2014, http://badatsports.com/2014/drawing-lines-of-communication-a-conversation-with-tony-lewis/.
4. Sol LeWitt, "Paragraphs on Conceptual Art," *Artforum* 5, no. 10 (Summer 1967): 79–84.
5. Ibid., 80.
6. Tony Lewis, email to Betsy Johnson, February 9, 2022.
7. Ibid.
8. Ibid.
9. "Many of the passages [of *Life's Little Instruction Book*] are really clichéd and painfully mundane, but true. Being able to use it as a source to make work allows me to have some sort of distance from it. It's satire, but there is also a belief in the words. This initial tension is where the project begins, and then drawings can go in other places." Tony Lewis, "Tony Lewis's Epigrammatic Abstractions," *Inside/Within Web Archive* (December 2014), http://insidewithin.com/tony-lewis/.
10. Tony Lewis, "In Conversation: Tony Lewis & Hamza Walker," Blum & Poe, Los Angeles, June 29, 2019, https://vimeo.com/364533643.

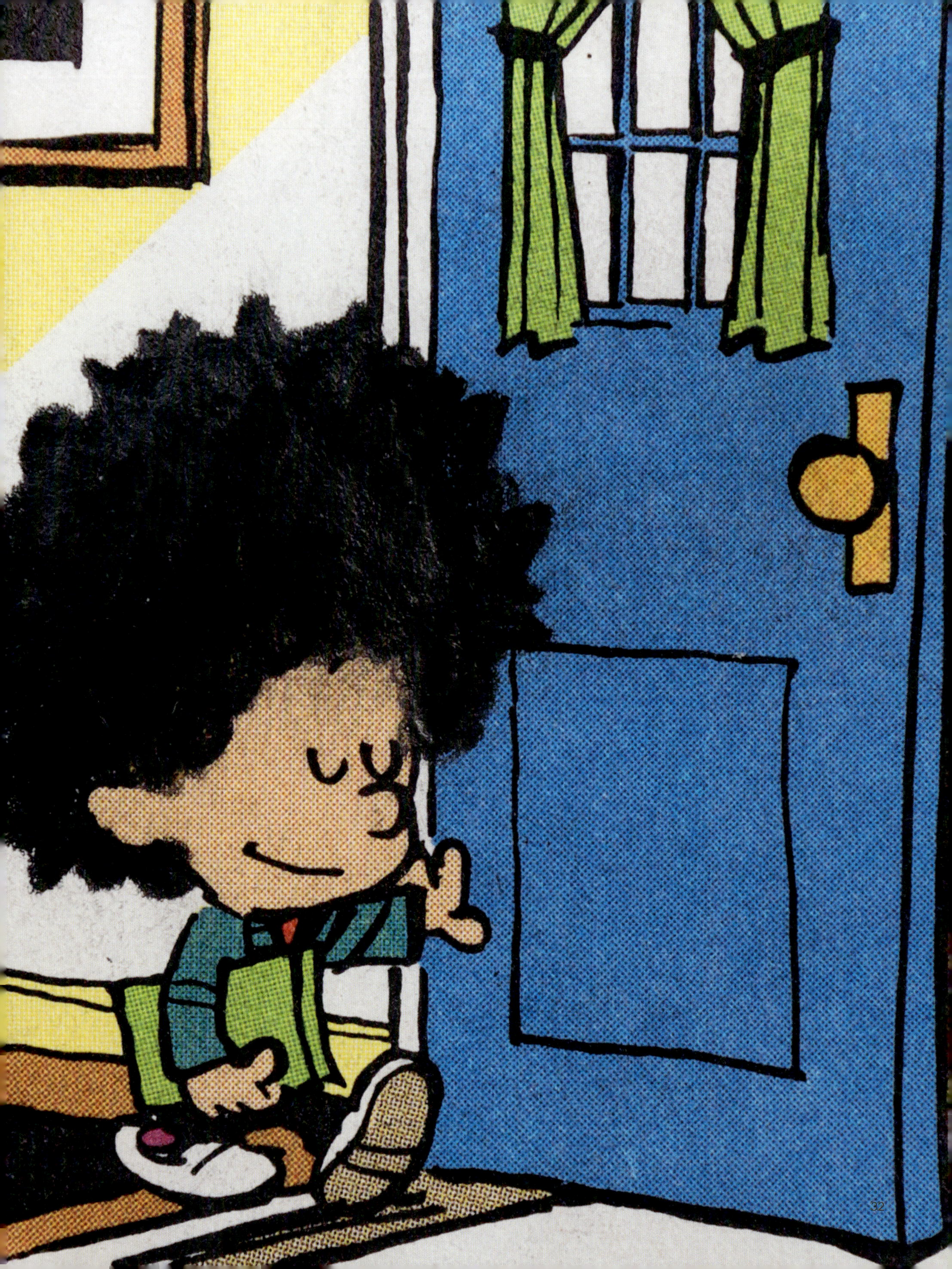

DEAR MR. W.

Tony Lewis

Dear Mr. Watterson,

My name is Tony Lewis, and I'm an artist and a lifelong fan of your work. First, I'd like to thank you for taking the time to read this letter, should it ever cross your path. I've been working for years to build up the courage to write you, and I believe this book is a good opportunity to do it. Second, I'd like to thank you for giving the world *Calvin and Hobbes*. It is one of the most inspirational pieces of art I've encountered in my life. It came to me as a child growing up in the suburbs of Cleveland, Ohio, and it stuck with me through my undergraduate life near Pittsburgh. Most notably, it has enhanced my understanding of my adult self as I received my MFA and became a full-time professional artist in Chicago. It's safe to say that since fourth grade, not a week has gone by that I haven't read, thought about, commented on, or remembered the greatness of *Calvin and Hobbes*. I'm probably not the loudest fan in the world, but I'm a fierce and loyal one.

It's hard to encapsulate the impact your work has had on mine. In some ways, your work was my first conception of a text-based art—the definition of which has since been expanded exponentially by my education—yet, in the present moment of my understanding, your work continues to hit the nail on the head. To me, you stand with Lawrence Weiner, Barbara Kruger, Glenn Ligon, Jenny Holzer, Stéphane Mallarmé, and Adrian Piper, among others whose work paved the way for my practice.

It's important to note that I'm a self-identifying Black contemporary artist with a deep commitment to language and drawing, both in a broad sense. For the past ten years, I've developed a studio practice that is

Fig. 1. Tony Lewis, *Untitled (Calvin Walking Outside with a Green Book/Box)*, 2014. Pencil and graphite on book page; 2 3/8 × 2 1/16 in. (6.1 × 5.2 cm)

fully committed to finding new ways to make drawings. Language, as I see it, functions as a tool to help me build and organize different types of drawings, with a wide range of subject matter. I've committed myself to a physically intense studio investigation of graphite powder, pencil, and paper in many forms over the years. I've been fortunate to have had several solo and group exhibitions nationally and internationally, most notably *Tony Lewis: Anthology 2014–2016*, a solo exhibition at the Hirshhorn Museum and Sculpture Garden in 2018—the latter being the reason I'm writing to you. This book grew out of that show, and I would be infinitely humbled and grateful were you to someday read and respond to it.

To give you a bit more background on who I am: in 2001, when I was in ninth grade at Orange High School in Pepper Pike, Ohio, my father gifted me a copy of *The Authoritative Calvin and Hobbes* after I received a 95 percent on a Western Civilization exam. That book changed my life, gave me confidence, and made me a better student. It was my first legitimate collection of the strip that I hadn't stolen from my sister, and I never looked back. That very book stayed with me for years, and over time I was able to find several secondhand copies of *Yukon Ho!*, *Weirdos from Another Planet!*, and others at thrift stores in Maple Heights, all of which followed me to Chicago. The original gift from my dad carried special meaning, as well as a few rips and bruises after I'd spent years thumbing through the pages. It quickly became one of the most precious objects I had ever brought into my studio, and the decision to take it there immediately changed my relationship to it. Here I was, with two of the most meaningful things I possessed to date: this fourteen-year-old copy of *The Authoritative Calvin and Hobbes* and a five-year-old studio practice that I'd worked so hard to build (fig. 2).

It was at this moment that I started to look back and reevaluate the more influential literary inspirations

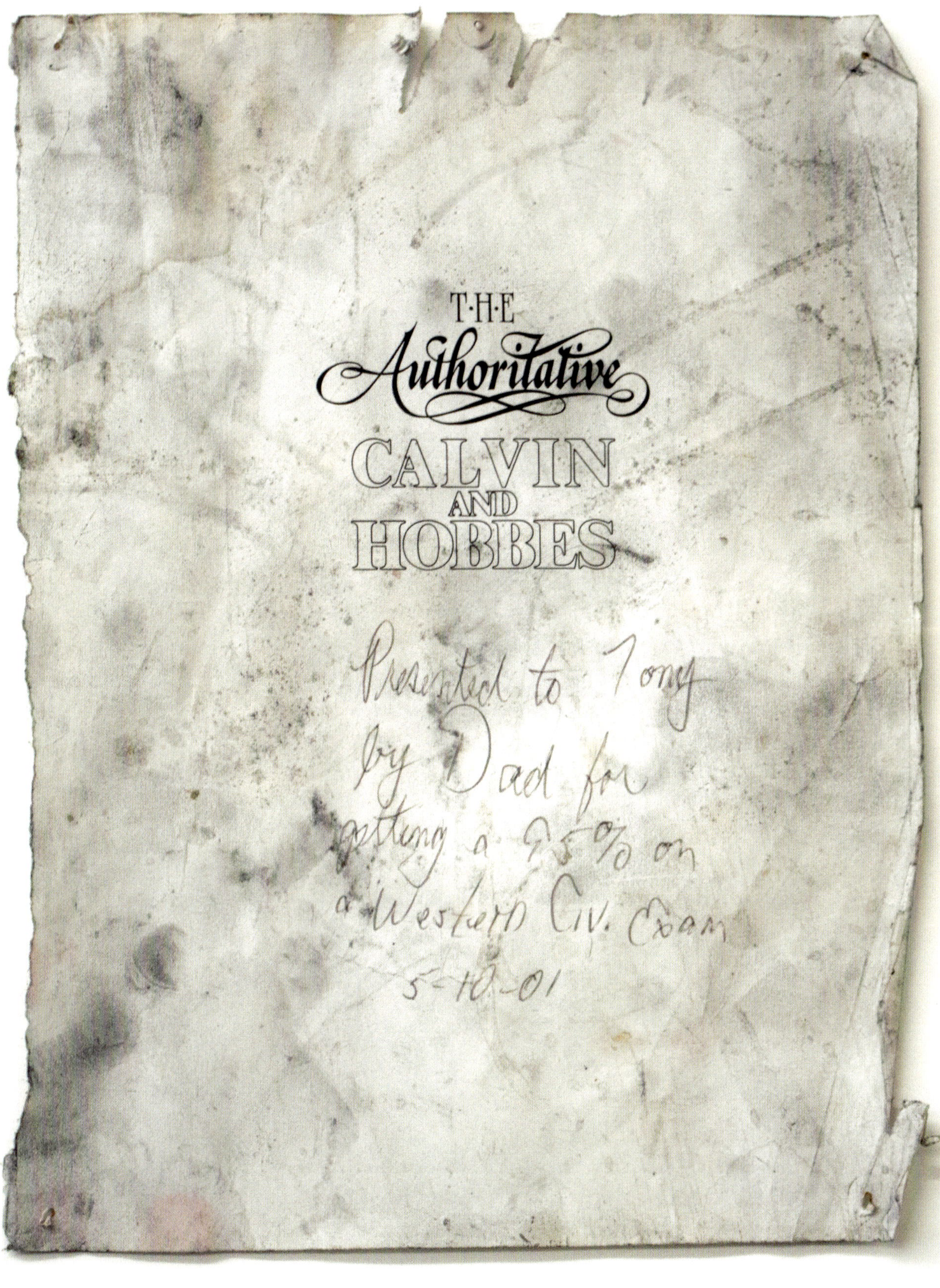

Fig. 2. Title page, Bill Watterson, *The Authoritative Calvin and Hobbes* (Kansas City, MO: Andrews McMeel, 1990), inscribed by Tony Lewis's father, 2001

in my life—the *Life's Little Instruction Book* series, by H. Jackson Brown Jr.; all of *Calvin and Hobbes*; the Bible; and others—to try to understand my development of self-worth, humor, and the adolescent lexicon that I still employ today. Bringing these childhood memories into the studio gave me a personal subject matter within my drawings, and it allowed me to gain a new perspective on those memories as an adult.

I've become increasingly interested in what art (and specifically drawing) can do to help people learn more about themselves and their history. I think that's what happened for me when I combined my enduring love of *Calvin and Hobbes* with my self-realized passion for drawing: I started to learn about myself. I began altering the book my father gave me, and I began drawing on it. It immediately felt blasphemous, not only because of my love for the strip, but also because I felt like I was throwing away a symbol of educational achievement that I had kept and cherished for so long. Equally, and surprisingly, it was one of the most liberating acts I could have undertaken for myself. In that moment, through the act of drawing, I felt closer than ever to *Calvin and Hobbes*. Not until I started drawing on the actual paper of the strip was I able to completely see myself in the vast, playful, and imaginative narrative I'd grown to love. I also realized, in that same instant, that the paper itself had changed from a beloved strip to a small, conceptual, graphite-on-paper drawing that began to carry a much deeper, personal meaning: I discovered, for the first time in the studio, how to conflate my sacrilegious love of the comic strip with drawing as an act of self-realization.

I then used this way of making drawings to build random phrases (by placing the small drawings next to each other), and these phrases eventually took on a more succinct meaning and direction. This process became a pathway to creative writing and was materially solidified with collage—the literal additive process of applying a series of small "text drawings" to a substrate to create one body of writing. Given the range of meaning, brevity, and rhythm of the writing, poetry was the only way to describe what was happening. The studio effort ended with thirty-four of these collage-poems, which I titled *Anthology 2014–2016*.

In addition to the exhibition at the Hirshhorn, the true culmination of the work was a self-produced paperback book of poetry that presented the written product culled from the collages, which preceded this present book. The liberation of language from the object of the collage is by far the most essential component of the entire project. It's paramount that what's left at the end is essentially free language—free from my father's gift, free from the brilliant light of *Calvin and Hobbes* itself, and even free from the metaphorical intensity and harsh reality of my ongoing studio practice.

Below I'd like to share a few of my key memories, thoughts, and questions that I've had throughout the process of making these drawings. Whether you're still reading this or not, thank you.

When I was a young kid living in Woodmere, Ohio, on Chagrin Boulevard, my mind was solely focused on Bone Thugs-N-Harmony, Laffy Taffy, and *Something under the Bed Is Drooling*. The first time I was called a nigger by a classmate was in fifth grade while I was playing mumball, which was right around the time I took *Revenge of the Baby-Sat* from my sister.

I knew Calvin was white, but for some reason he didn't seem racist. Maybe it was because I had decided that he wasn't. He and Hobbes were just hilarious, and just as ridiculous as me and my sister. There was always a feeling that we played in the same Metroparks, maybe went to the same school, and loved the same baseball team, but we didn't live in the same neighborhood. I would think about whether his parents would accept me if I went over to his house to play. They seemed like they would, but so had other parents who didn't.

Despite my inability to see my full self—by which I mean a young Black kid with hair or problems like mine—in the comic strip, I've always wanted to be on the same page as *Calvin and Hobbes*. I've always wanted to be that funny and introspective. I've always looked to be that inventive and ridiculous, but at ten years old, I didn't have the capacity to understand the difference between wanting all of those characteristics for myself and wanting simply to be a six-year-old white kid, an only child with a stuffed tiger and a nurtured, seemingly limitless imagination.

Three questions for you:

1. Did you ever consider nonwhite children as part of your audience when making the strip? If so, did that influence how you built the narratives or the jokes?
2. Speaking within the mind of Calvin, do you think there's space to understand difference between people? One of the first instances of this might be his relationship to his neighbor Susie, which I think played out as an archetypal show of white American boyhood. How do you think he would've reacted with a young Black friend or a Korean friend?
3. Did Calvin's whiteness seem problematic for you as a creator at any point? Has your understanding of the strip changed at all over the years in terms of the diversity of its audience?

My questions are not an indictment, or the beginning of a reckoning. It might seem that way because the only adoration I personally can give is Black adoration. I have to express love the only way I know how—through a Black American perspective. The questions might seem to challenge the existence of *Calvin and Hobbes*, and the legendary status it has. On the contrary, they are simply exposing the heights of its greatness, highlighting the expansive definition of its readership's adoration, and attempting to connect the beauty of the work to the reality of the world it changes. *Calvin and Hobbes* has had a profound, positive influence on Black youth—I am living proof.

The greatness of the strip is defined not only by every young white person who has been able to see their self within it, but also by every young nonwhite person who has not. Both people can still love the strip, but the way they learn to love *Calvin and Hobbes* is in part based on how the strip itself acknowledges and loves them back, which is entirely different for each one. It's not simply acknowledging lack of representation—that's a diagnosis. The true subject is damage control, the literal math after the trauma—what it's like to continually pick up the pieces of a nonexistent or scattered self-image to build a makeshift foundation of love for the self and then eventually for *Calvin and Hobbes*—that's the miracle. That love is intrinsic to the legacy of the strip, which continues to penetrate the hearts of a wide range of children and adults, showing them genuine humor and true friendship, sometimes for the first time. I currently work as one person looking back on the development of my own psychology, constantly asking questions I didn't have the language to form back then.

In whatever way my definition of love (which is to say Black love) was/is developing, a large portion of it is still given to *Calvin and Hobbes*. Thank you.

Sincerely,
Tony Lewis

DRAWINGS FOR TONY LEWIS

Karl Haendel

As the concept for this book evolved, it became clear that it would benefit from a contribution by someone who, like Tony, could communicate from the intersection of text and drawing. Tony approached Karl Haendel, a close friend whom Tony met in 2010 when Karl was a graduate advisor at the School of the Art Institute of Chicago. The two bonded over a shared enthusiasm for graphite, language, and conceptual drawing. Karl graciously agreed to participate, and as they began talking about what his contribution would look like, Karl realized that what needed to be said actually needed to be drawn. The following visual essay stems from many intimate emails, phone conversations, and texts. It's a fitting record of a twelve-year friendship rooted in curiosity, mentorship, brutal honesty, and, above all, an unhealthy commitment to drawing.

Karl Haendel (b. New York City, 1976), *Drawings for Tony Lewis*, 2021. Pencil on paper, 5 sheets; 30 × 22 in. (76.2 × 55.9 cm) each

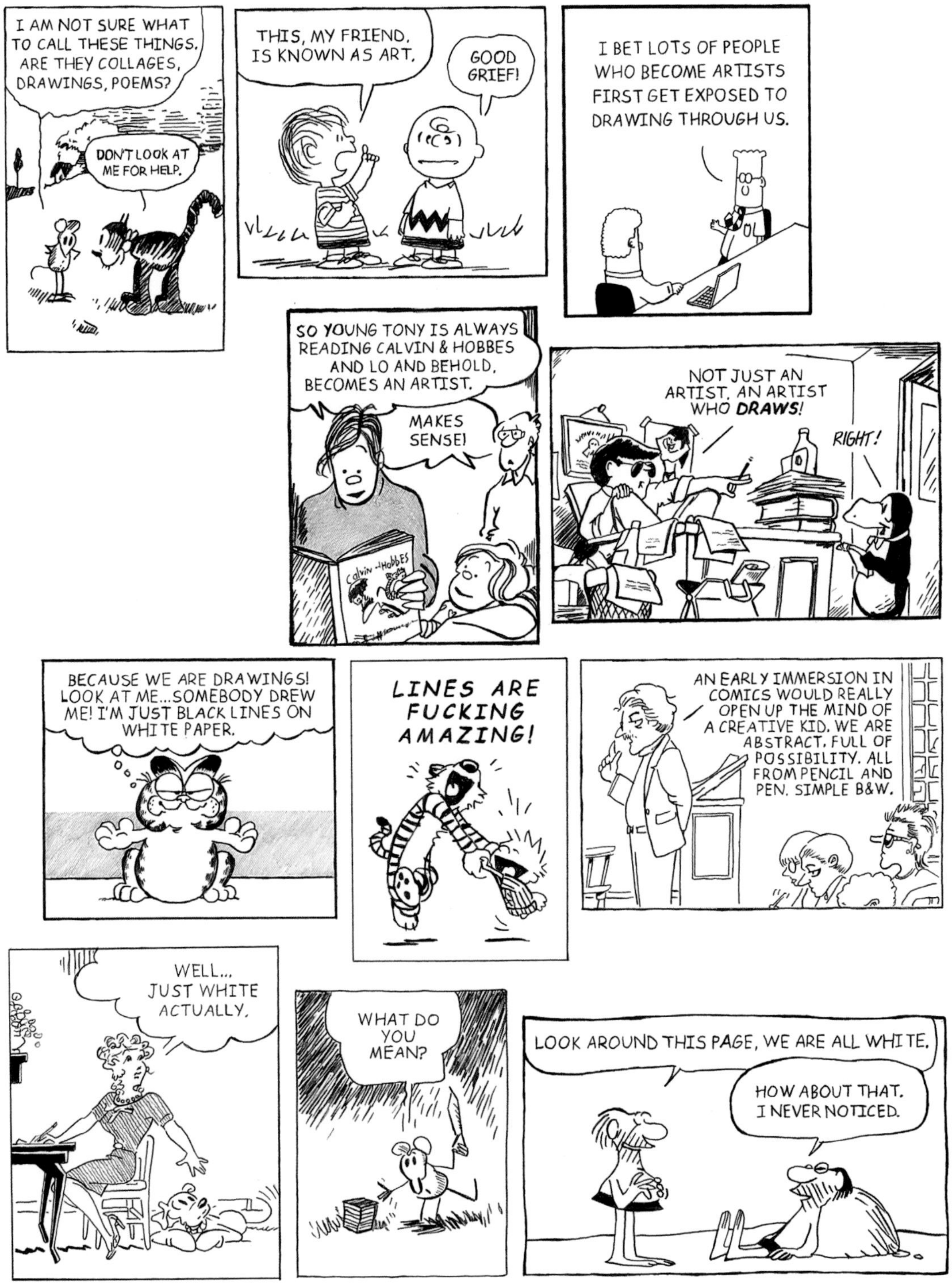
I AM NOT SURE WHAT TO CALL THESE THINGS. ARE THEY COLLAGES, DRAWINGS, POEMS?
DON'T LOOK AT ME FOR HELP.
THIS, MY FRIEND, IS KNOWN AS ART.
GOOD GRIEF!
I BET LOTS OF PEOPLE WHO BECOME ARTISTS FIRST GET EXPOSED TO DRAWING THROUGH US.
SO YOUNG TONY IS ALWAYS READING CALVIN & HOBBES AND LO AND BEHOLD, BECOMES AN ARTIST.
MAKES SENSE!
Calvin and Hobbes
NOT JUST AN ARTIST, AN ARTIST WHO DRAWS!
RIGHT!
BECAUSE WE ARE DRAWINGS! LOOK AT ME...SOMEBODY DREW ME! I'M JUST BLACK LINES ON WHITE PAPER.
LINES ARE FUCKING AMAZING!
AN EARLY IMMERSION IN COMICS WOULD REALLY OPEN UP THE MIND OF A CREATIVE KID. WE ARE ABSTRACT, FULL OF POSSIBILITY. ALL FROM PENCIL AND PEN. SIMPLE B&W.
WELL... JUST WHITE ACTUALLY.
WHAT DO YOU MEAN?
LOOK AROUND THIS PAGE, WE ARE ALL WHITE.
HOW ABOUT THAT. I NEVER NOTICED.

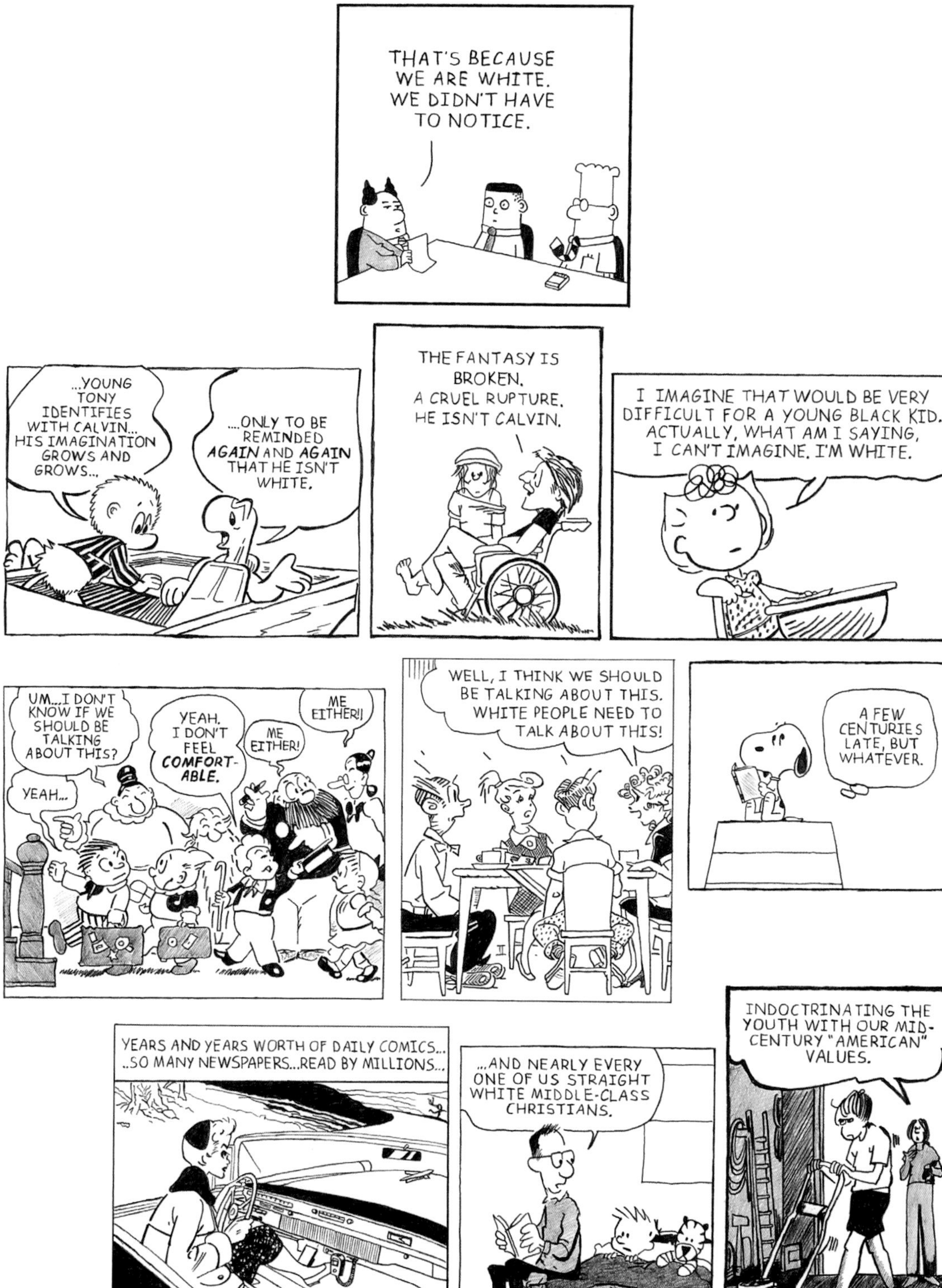
THAT'S BECAUSE WE ARE WHITE. WE DIDN'T HAVE TO NOTICE.
...YOUNG TONY IDENTIFIES WITH CALVIN... HIS IMAGINATION GROWS AND GROWS...
....ONLY TO BE REMINDED **AGAIN** AND **AGAIN** THAT HE ISN'T WHITE.
THE FANTASY IS BROKEN. A CRUEL RUPTURE. HE ISN'T CALVIN.
I IMAGINE THAT WOULD BE VERY DIFFICULT FOR A YOUNG BLACK KID. ACTUALLY, WHAT AM I SAYING, I CAN'T IMAGINE. I'M WHITE.
UM...I DON'T KNOW IF WE SHOULD BE TALKING ABOUT THIS?
YEAH...
YEAH. I DON'T FEEL **COMFORT-ABLE.**
ME EITHER!
ME EITHER!!
WELL, I THINK WE SHOULD BE TALKING ABOUT THIS. WHITE PEOPLE NEED TO TALK ABOUT THIS!
A FEW CENTURIES LATE, BUT WHATEVER.
YEARS AND YEARS WORTH OF DAILY COMICS... ..SO MANY NEWSPAPERS...READ BY MILLIONS...
...AND NEARLY EVERY ONE OF US STRAIGHT WHITE MIDDLE-CLASS CHRISTIANS.
INDOCTRINATING THE YOUTH WITH OUR MID-CENTURY "AMERICAN" VALUES.

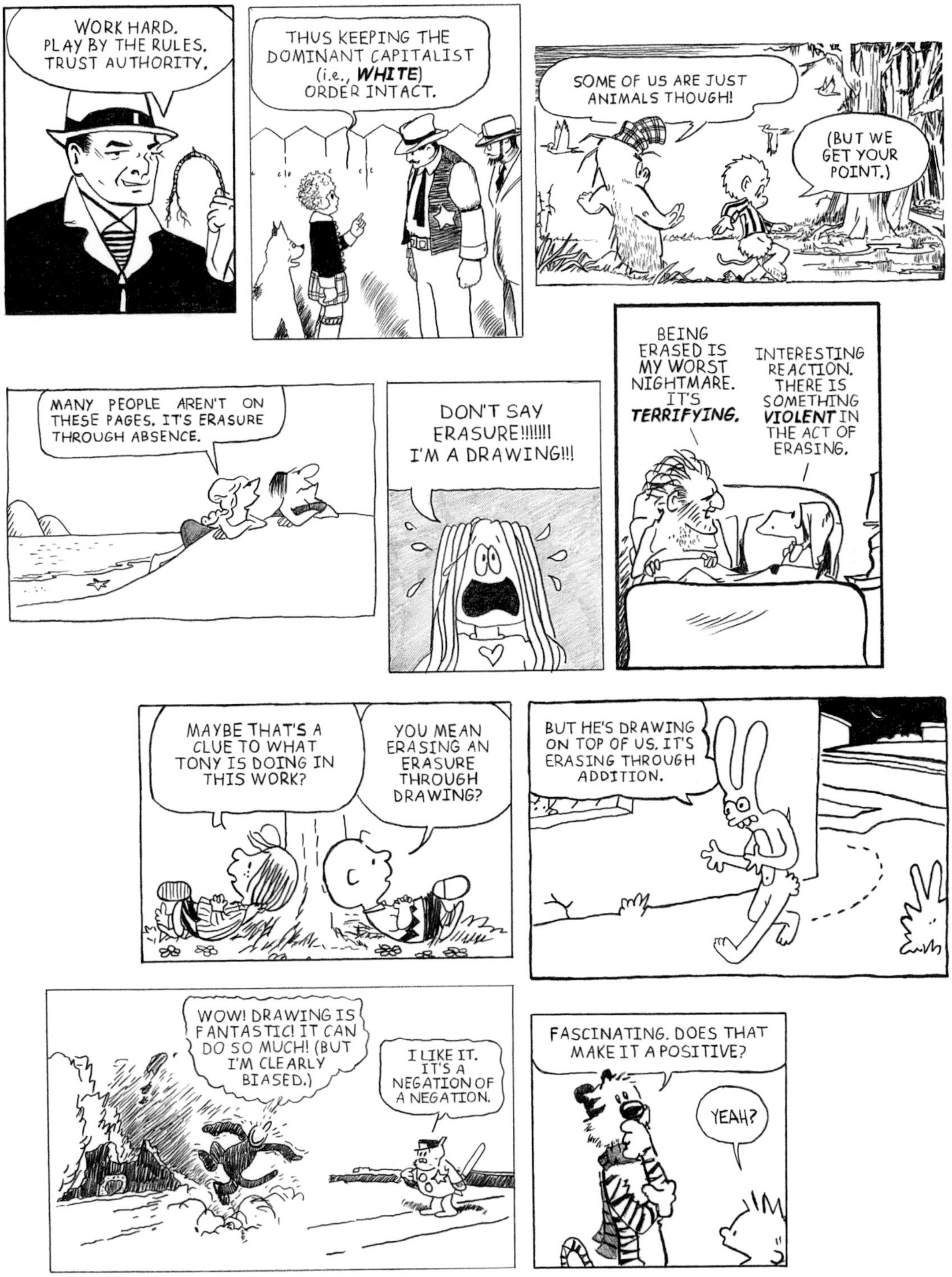
WORK HARD. PLAY BY THE RULES. TRUST AUTHORITY.
THUS KEEPING THE DOMINANT CAPITALIST (i.e., **WHITE**) ORDER INTACT.
SOME OF US ARE JUST ANIMALS THOUGH!
(BUT WE GET YOUR POINT.)
MANY PEOPLE AREN'T ON THESE PAGES. IT'S ERASURE THROUGH ABSENCE.
DON'T SAY ERASURE!!!!!! I'M A DRAWING!!!
BEING ERASED IS MY WORST NIGHTMARE. IT'S ***TERRIFYING.***
INTERESTING REACTION. THERE IS SOMETHING **VIOLENT** IN THE ACT OF ERASING.
MAYBE THAT'S A CLUE TO WHAT TONY IS DOING IN THIS WORK?
YOU MEAN ERASING AN ERASURE THROUGH DRAWING?
BUT HE'S DRAWING ON TOP OF US. IT'S ERASING THROUGH ADDITION.
WOW! DRAWING IS FANTASTIC! IT CAN DO SO MUCH! (BUT I'M CLEARLY BIASED.)
I LIKE IT. IT'S A NEGATION OF A NEGATION.
FASCINATING. DOES THAT MAKE IT A POSITIVE?
YEAH?

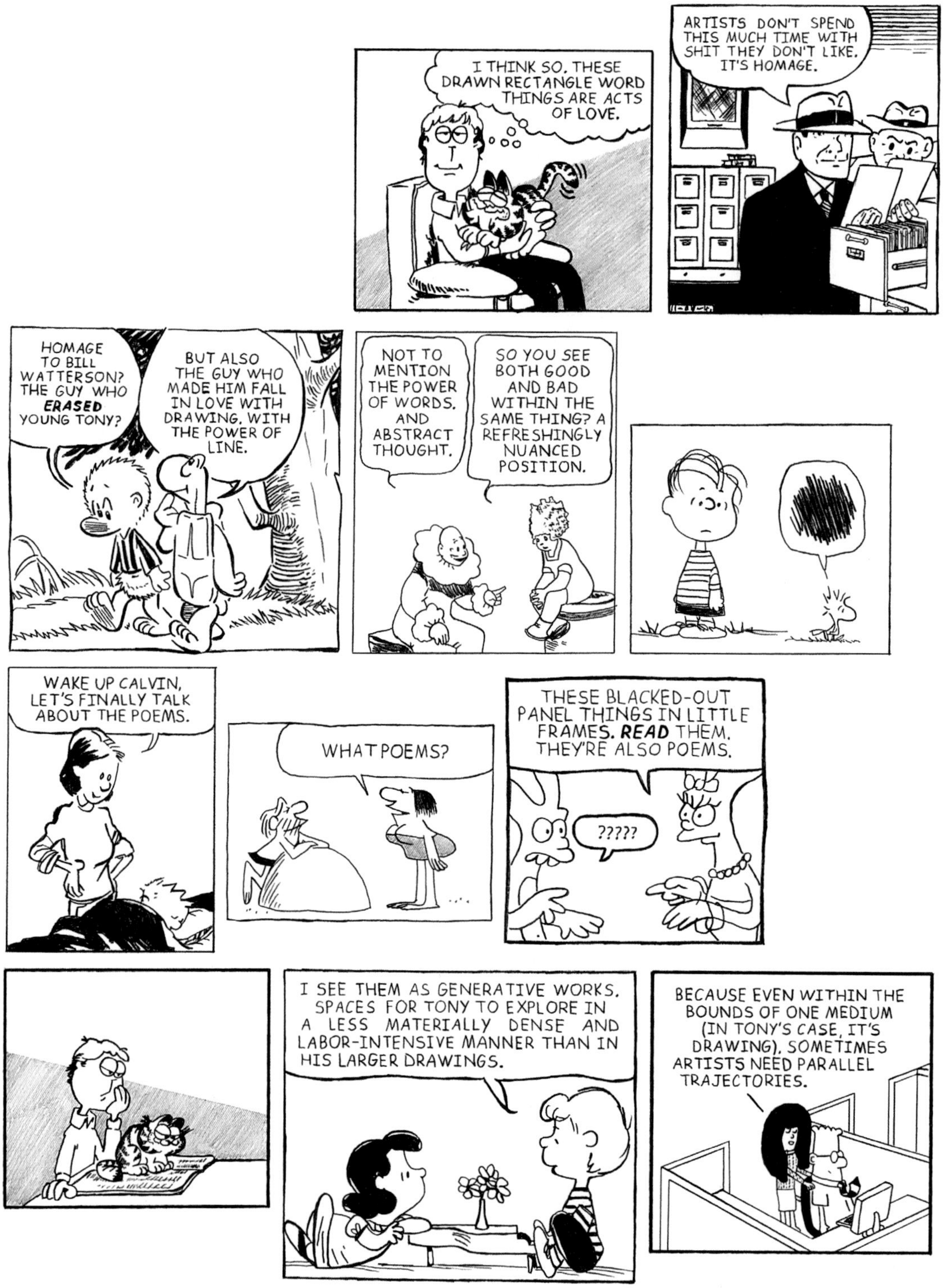

I THINK SO. THESE DRAWN RECTANGLE WORD THINGS ARE ACTS OF LOVE.
ARTISTS DON'T SPEND THIS MUCH TIME WITH SHIT THEY DON'T LIKE. IT'S HOMAGE.
HOMAGE TO BILL WATTERSON? THE GUY WHO ERASED YOUNG TONY?
BUT ALSO THE GUY WHO MADE HIM FALL IN LOVE WITH DRAWING, WITH THE POWER OF LINE.
NOT TO MENTION THE POWER OF WORDS. AND ABSTRACT THOUGHT.
SO YOU SEE BOTH GOOD AND BAD WITHIN THE SAME THING? A REFRESHINGLY NUANCED POSITION.
WAKE UP CALVIN, LET'S FINALLY TALK ABOUT THE POEMS.
WHAT POEMS?
THESE BLACKED-OUT PANEL THINGS IN LITTLE FRAMES. READ THEM. THEY'RE ALSO POEMS.
?????
I SEE THEM AS GENERATIVE WORKS. SPACES FOR TONY TO EXPLORE IN A LESS MATERIALLY DENSE AND LABOR-INTENSIVE MANNER THAN IN HIS LARGER DRAWINGS.
BECAUSE EVEN WITHIN THE BOUNDS OF ONE MEDIUM (IN TONY'S CASE, IT'S DRAWING), SOMETIMES ARTISTS NEED PARALLEL TRAJECTORIES.

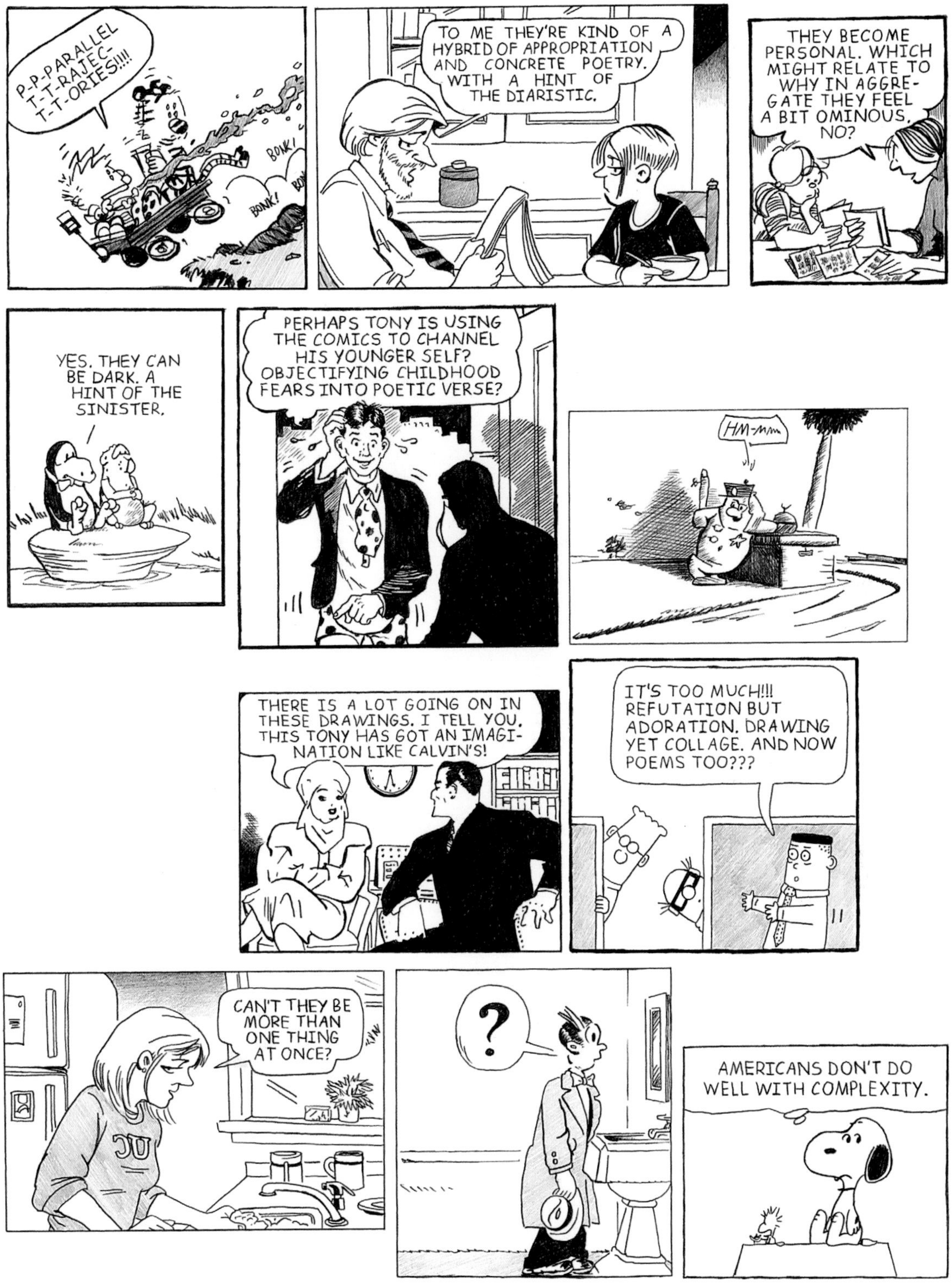
P-P-PARALLEL T-T-RAJEC-T-T-ORIES!!!!
BONK!
BONK!
TO ME THEY'RE KIND OF A HYBRID OF APPROPRIATION AND CONCRETE POETRY. WITH A HINT OF THE DIARISTIC.
THEY BECOME PERSONAL. WHICH MIGHT RELATE TO WHY IN AGGREGATE THEY FEEL A BIT OMINOUS, NO?
YES. THEY CAN BE DARK. A HINT OF THE SINISTER.
PERHAPS TONY IS USING THE COMICS TO CHANNEL HIS YOUNGER SELF? OBJECTIFYING CHILDHOOD FEARS INTO POETIC VERSE?
HM-mm
THERE IS A LOT GOING ON IN THESE DRAWINGS. I TELL YOU, THIS TONY HAS GOT AN IMAGINATION LIKE CALVIN'S!
IT'S TOO MUCH!!! REFUTATION BUT ADORATION. DRAWING YET COLLAGE. AND NOW POEMS TOO???
CAN'T THEY BE MORE THAN ONE THING AT ONCE?
?
AMERICANS DON'T DO WELL WITH COMPLEXITY.

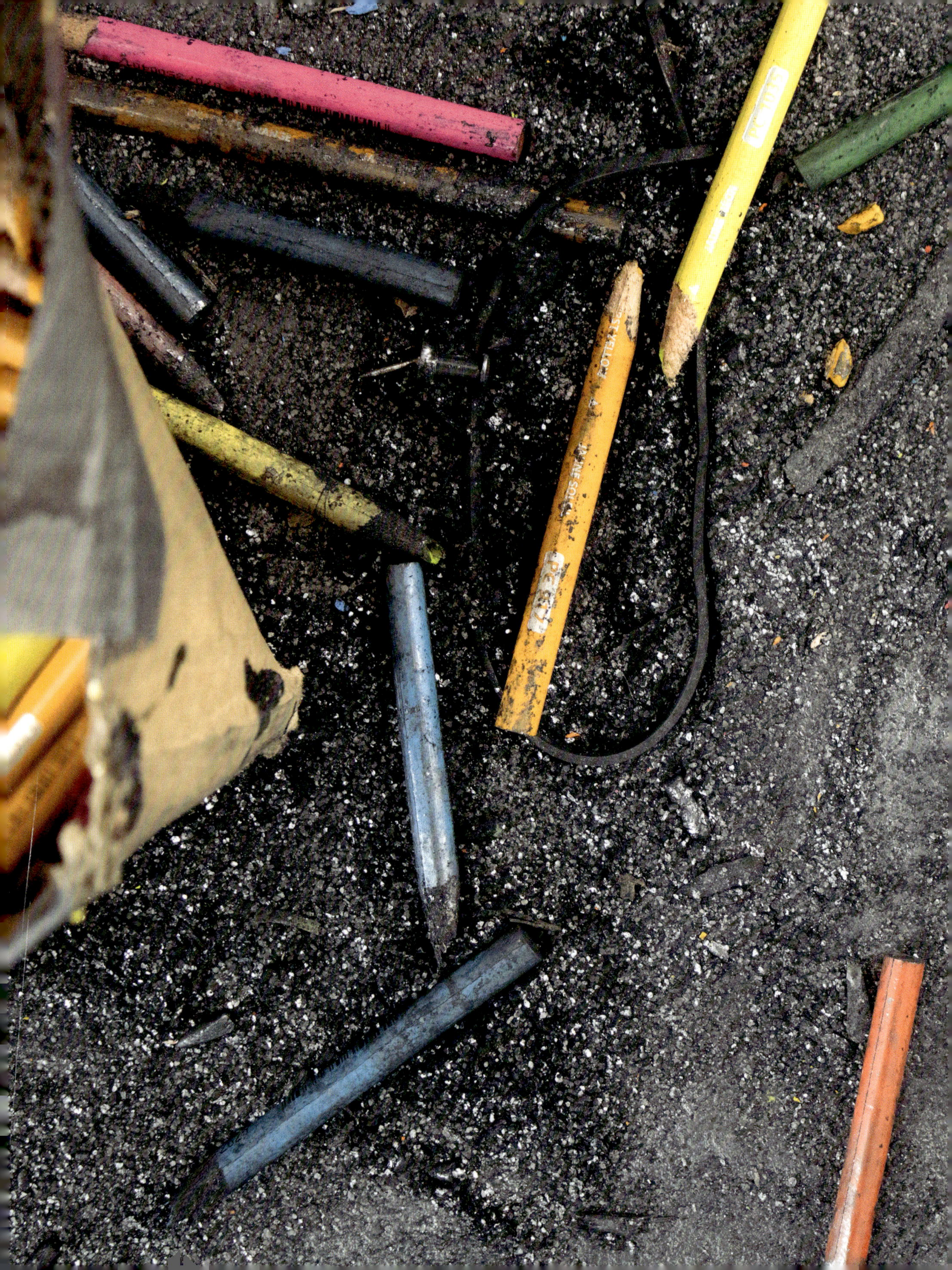

TONY LEWIS
IN AND OUT OF CODE
Theaster Gates

It was the studio's slipperiness and low light that made my first encounter with it immediately off-centering—its fluorescence and shadows against a floor layered with graphite and formerly stark white paper darkened through trespass made me feel as if I had just entered an immersive sculpture, not a laboratory for crafting drawings. I understood immediately that Tony Lewis's bodies of language-based drawings are indicative of a way of thinking as much as they are a way of working. *Brief, prune, initialism, abridgment, reduction, truncation, shorthand, DRAWING*: these are the words that passed through my head during this first encounter. In one work, a long, right-leaning loop is followed by a horizontal line, a descending C-like shape, and two dashes (fig. 2). It's like Gregg shorthand; it's a challenge because all the vowels are gone. But they show up in other works: *ooooooo, ooooooo.* tears across another drawing (fig. 3), and somewhere in all those *O*s are *People of Color* (fig. 4) and other words, some revealed, some not, some off the page altogether.

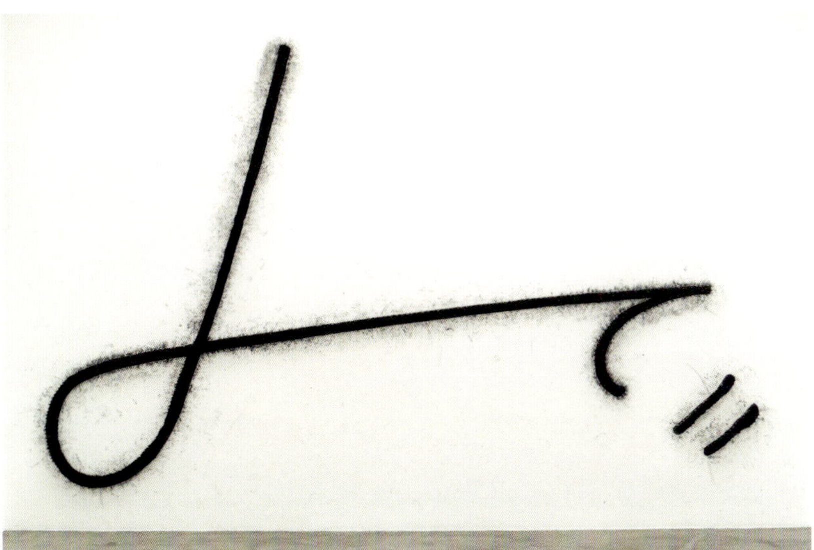

Fig. 2. Tony Lewis, *"What is dangerous here is a turning away from . . . the turning away from . . . anything any white American says. . . . But I don't know, and neither does Martin Luther King—none of us know—how to deal with those other people . . . who don't believe anything the white world says, and don't entirely believe anything I or Martin say,"* 2019. Graphite powder, screws, and rubber bands; dimensions variable. Installation view, *Charlatan and Ultimately a Boring Man*, Blum & Poe, Los Angeles, 2019

Fig. 1. Tony Lewis's studio floor, 2022

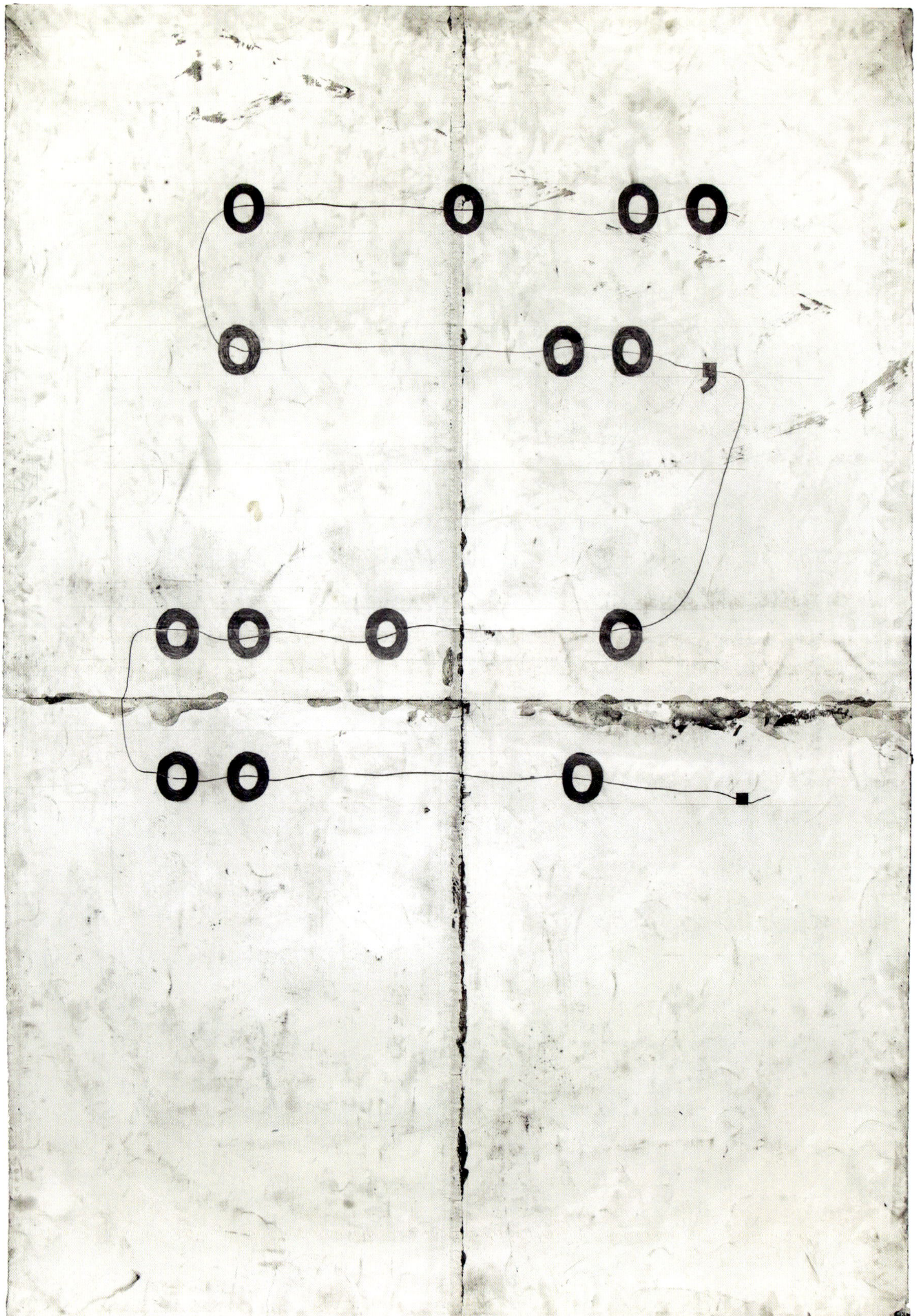

Fig. 3. Tony Lewis, *ooooooo, ooooooo.*, 2011. Pencil and graphite powder on paper; 84 × 60 in. (213.4 × 152.4 cm)

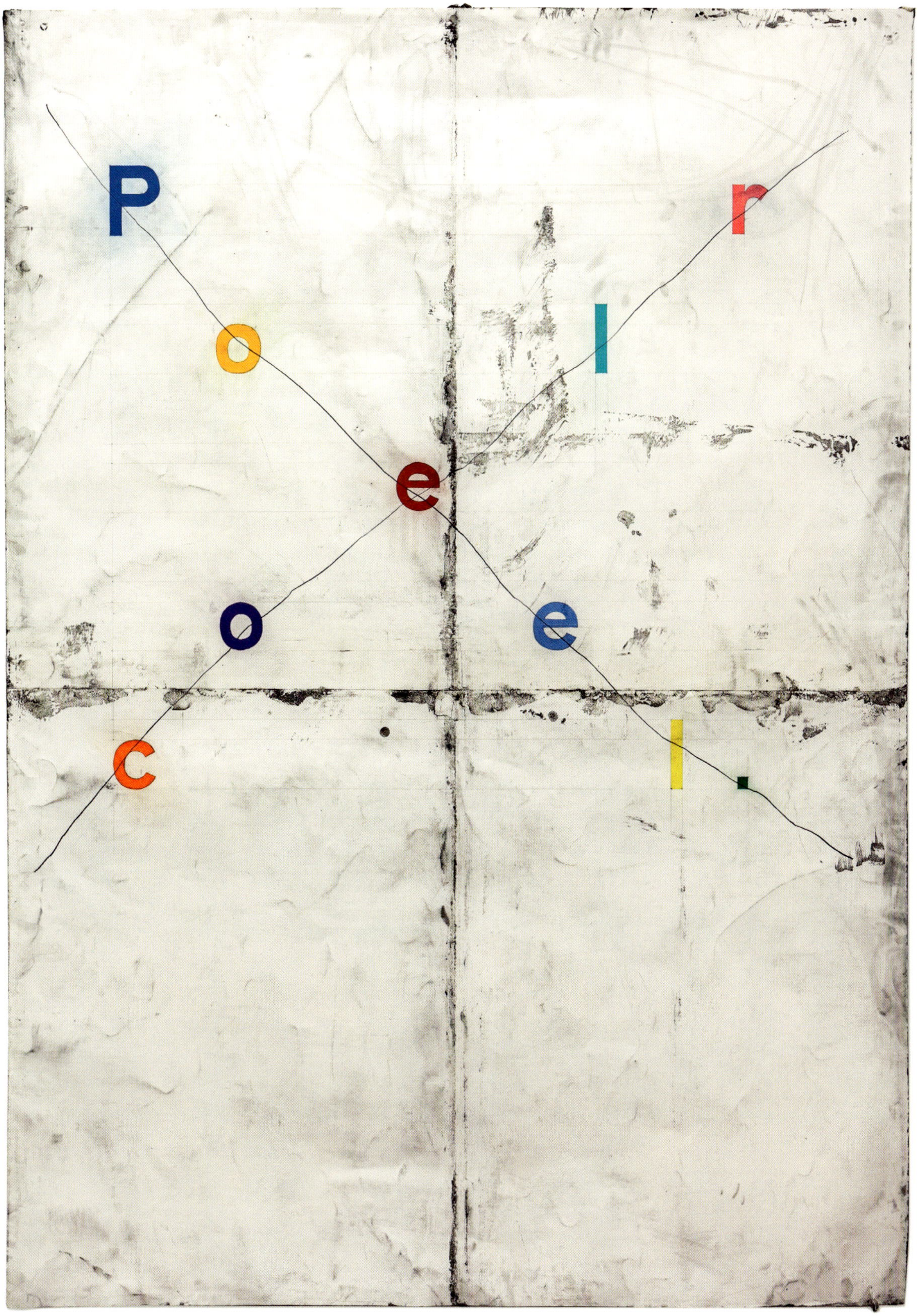

Fig. 4. Tony Lewis, *X*, 2019. Pencil, colored pencil, and graphite powder on paper; 84 × 60 in. (213.4 × 152.4 cm)

I remember those *O*s from the summer of 2012, when I first saw them on the floor of Lewis's studio. *O*s everywhere, and other vowels on other pages, like a low-fi/analog *Wheel of Fortune*. I found myself attempting to understand the meaning of the works by reading the drawings as they were presented to me and feeling the movement of sounds and graphite on the page. It was literary and material poetry, redacted and revealed; the series of breaks between vowels felt at once fully resolved and intentionally withheld. Both drawing and language were familiar and new. The work did not offer a solution to a question; it seemed more like a declaration of resistance, wrapped in graphite and unavailable. I tried to utter all the sounds as a performance, but what emerged seemed more like an episode of aphasia than something creative. There was loss represented on the page, not just the loss of the missing language but an intentional loss that was hiding or offering something else. The marks, which seemed both fully alphabetical and transmuted into shorthand, were withholdings of language, or, better, shortenings that were preparing me to know and not know.

Lewis has often shared how athletic his process is in the studio, and the physical nature of the work was immediately evident. Not in monumental overtures of line, but in the painstaking effort he had exerted to produce these drawings that reveal an intention more investigative than it is declarative. I understood immediately that Lewis's earliest bodies of language-based drawings were indicative of a way of thinking as much as they were a way of working. He was *speaking*.

Many make marks that begin with something much more (if not absolutely) emotional than Lewis does. Instead he builds word worlds: he revels in the complexity of language. Even when his work is in front of your face, your quest to understand it goes unanswered, like Braille, unless you know its codes. When I first saw these striking gestures, they seemed very much like an indecipherable puzzle. I remember pondering how much

Lewis wanted to share (knowledge) and whether he was preoccupied with "understanding" in his paintings or with completely obscuring his subjective secrets (fig. 5). For me, at least, Lewis's work has shaped my own path toward abstraction, especially language-based abstraction. The work's restraint is a first indicator of its maker. Lewis is completely present, humorous, and human—and absolutely private, reserved, and decorous. The paintings allude to this availability as well as to his firm disregard for comprehension or comprehensiveness.

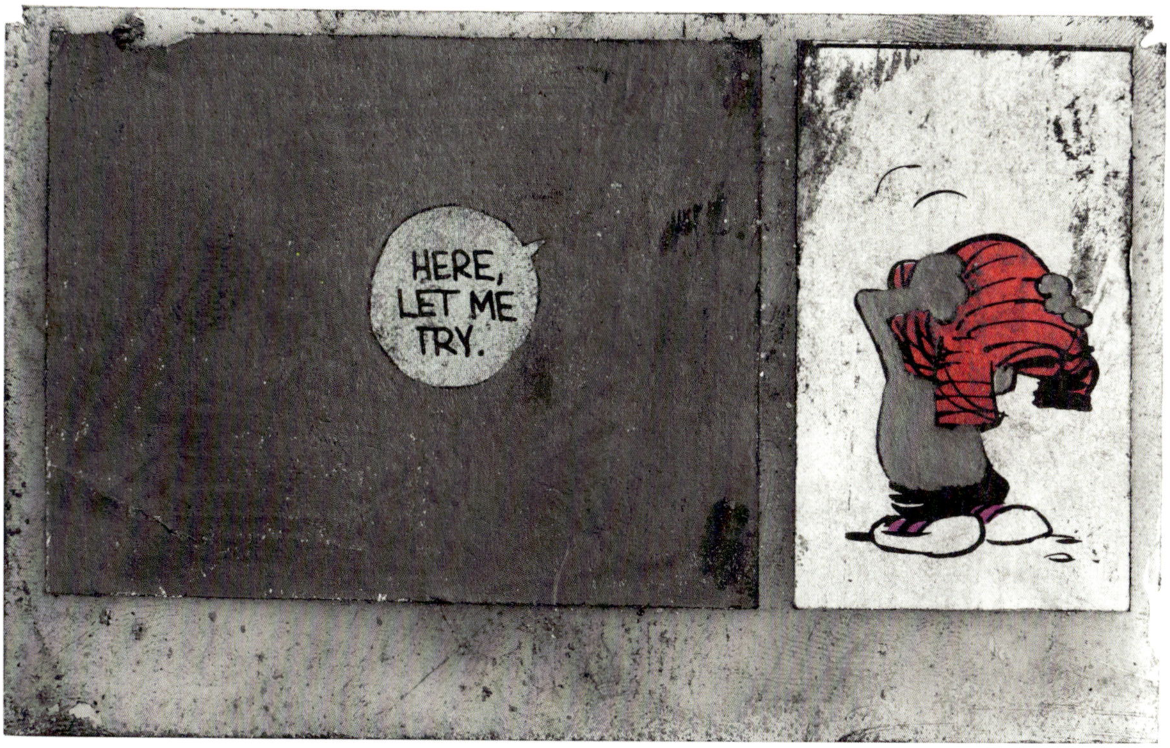

Fig. 5. Tony Lewis, *Untitled*, 2013. Pencil and graphite on book page; 2 1/16 × 4 3/4 in. (5.2 × 12.1 cm)

What seemed key in that first studio visit and my subsequent encounters with Lewis was the extreme synthesis that he demonstrates as he grapples with his interior world and his artistic preoccupations, which include language, the Western art canonical traditions, and new code forms. Lewis uses language to continue or even ignite conversations between his worlds, and the syncretistic effort necessary to unify such a diverse set of interests is realized through drawing. His syncretism envelops philosophy, youth culture, the American tragedies of racialized violence, the possibilities within artistic form, and a deep acknowledgment of the canon, in which Lewis clearly believes and of which he is clearly a part. The drawings are always revealing and restraining; through his substantial body of work, Lewis offers his hand and leaves space for codes. Codes come in many forms—language, rhythm, mark, and sound—and it is this way of investing in code that offers artistic and perhaps greater personal freedoms.

Coding is at the root of survival, especially when considered adjacent to servitude. To code is to be Black, with knowledge different from the master's or the state's knowledge. Blackness is born in code and has needed code for survival. To code is to know, to make the known unknowable, and then to know again through signs and symbols that are both perceptual and effectual. Symbols moved us through the historically subjugated terrain of the South by night years ago, and they move us through the complexities of contemporary life and artistic practice in this day. We have to grapple with our collective histories as Americans, our universal histories as humans, and our specific histories as people of color, blending them all into an amalgam of knowing and saying and speeching and signifying. To do this well is a kind of syncretistic intelligence and a deeply informed source of fulfillment, especially for Lewis.

I am reminded of the 1965 debate between James Baldwin and William Buckley at the University of Cambridge, transcripts and video footage of which Lewis used as the basis for a body of work titled *Charlatan and Ultimately a Boring Man* in 2019. When you watch the footage, it is evident from the very beginning that the oppositional rifts that exist around the debate's central question—the American Dream and its relationship to the "Negro"—not only were pertinent during the time of the debate but unfortunately are still relevant today. But for me, one of the most interesting points in the debate is a quite modest moment in its opening minutes, when Baldwin is speaking and laying the ideological groundwork for his defense of the Negro and the camera pans the audience to a Black man who is intensely watching. On his face is a stare so telling that it grabbed me deeply.

That stare is absolutely crucial to my reflections not only on Tony Lewis's work, but also on the place of contemporary artistic practices in the wake of Modernism. On this young scholar's face was excitement, anticipation of a great battle between two minds, and apprehension and anxiety as he, one of the few Black people in the audience, struggled to know the outcome of the battle. Our young Black Cambridge acolyte seemed held in a state of high anxiety because Baldwin's potential success or failure was, in some way, linked to his own.

As I watched this moment of tension over and over again, I tried to imagine that the debate was not just about the state of the Negro in America and whether the American Dream had been successful as a result of the Negro's labor, but also about the role language plays in determining the destiny of others. Language, with its many powers, can function as code, and these codes can and often do shape our belief in one another, our taste, and social understanding. In Tony Lewis, I see a maker of marks who understands and manages that power with intelligence and profound generosity.

The beauty of code is its possibility of deep communication and recognition across lines—between the oppressive state and the free state. The free state lives in a site of decipherability and the deep desire to be understood. To be in the free state is to be part of the system of understanding the latitude of knowledge through a wellspring of shared or mutual information. Code strategies help us survive and sometimes achieve success between the disruptions of difference, be they temporal, spatial, political, or cultural. The formal codes of drawing help us mark the terrain, giving cues from the interior to the North, from dark paths to future freedom seekers by way of a shout, cry, marking on a tree, or paper sheets made heavy with the weight of hot graphite (fig. 6), giving us constant syllabic cues that emerge from igneous reserves both near and far.

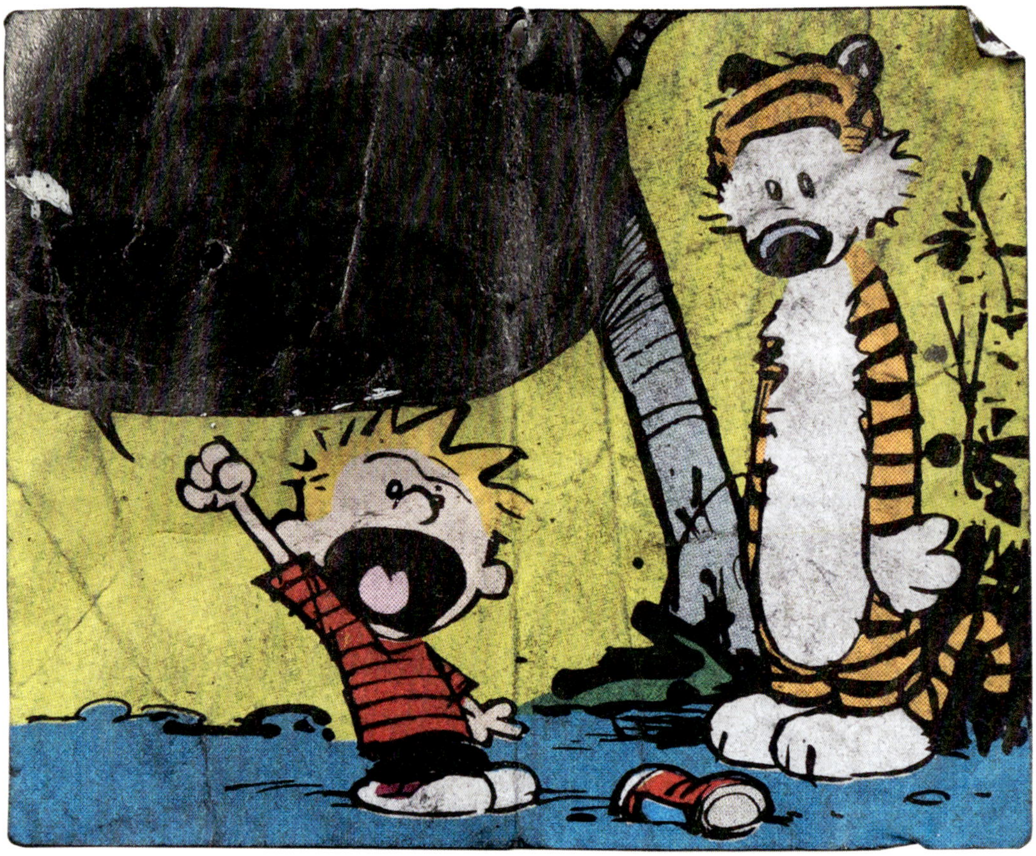

Fig. 6. Tony Lewis, *Untitled*, 2013. Pencil and graphite on book page; $2\frac{5}{8} \times 3\frac{3}{4}$ in. (6.7 × 9.5 cm)

The signifiers that produce new works are often birthed from the same pool of inherited social conditions. Artists ask (1) Why am I making this? (2) What am I trying to say about this? and (3) To whom do I wish to speak? For those who are able to create compelling reflections and have a sense of whom they are speaking to, making can be an exceptional forum for direct communication, a physical witness to an emotional act, a tempered promise that reverberates into the future. In Lewis's case, the paths toward communication are as sophisticated as they are straightforward. He finds a way with his work to shroud meaning in abstract marks and convince us through balance, ability, historical signifiers, and the intelligence of the determined gesture that "the call" is worth listening for and understanding or grappling with. It is this combination of literalness, perceptual invitation, and scale that gives us the sense that we are present at the birth of new language and witness to a holistic attempt to activate speech and knowledge through mark-making. What I am trying to describe is the usefulness of abstraction as a place to both hide and be seen. It is in this way that artists like Lewis expand, with clarity of intent, the possibilities of abstraction.

ANTHOLOGY 2014–2016

Plates 1–34. Tony Lewis (b. Los Angeles, California, 1986), *Anthology 2014–2016*, 2014–2016. Graphite, correction tape, and paper collage (comics) on transparency; 11 × 8½ in. (27.9 × 21.6 cm) each. Joseph H. Hirshhorn Purchase Fund, 2019 (2019.012.01–34)

Surface

Look hard, what putrid
Heavy
    Steaming thing. How
Mysterious
And
Brave
Rumbling
                    Into
A Volcano

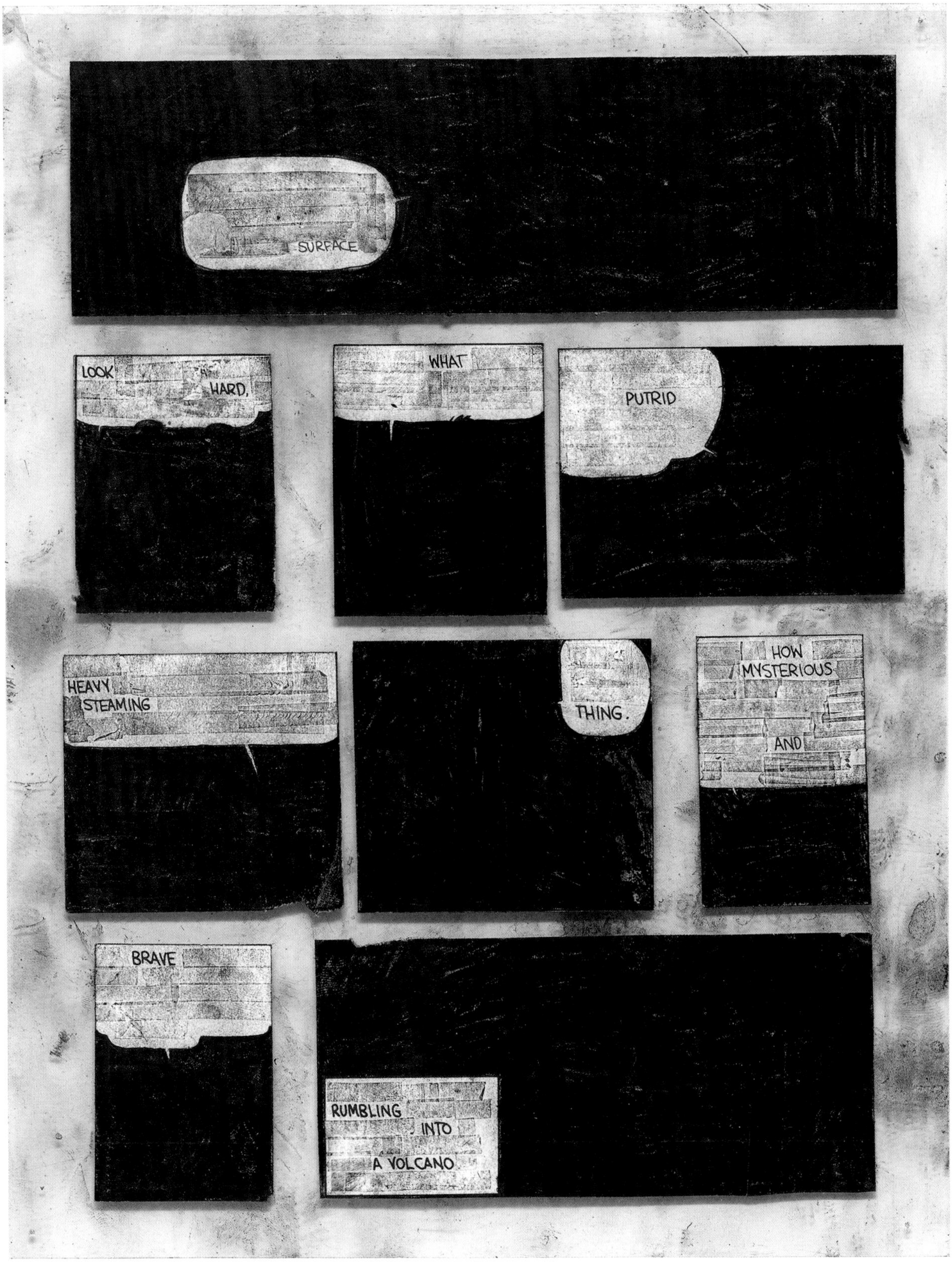
SURFACE
LOOK HARD,
WHAT
PUTRID
HEAVY STEAMING
THING.
HOW MYSTERIOUS
AND
BRAVE
RUMBLING INTO A VOLCANO

And

Give me a smile
There's nothing I
believe
                  More
Furiously. He
Downshifts
                  And . . .
Uh oh.
Nothing.

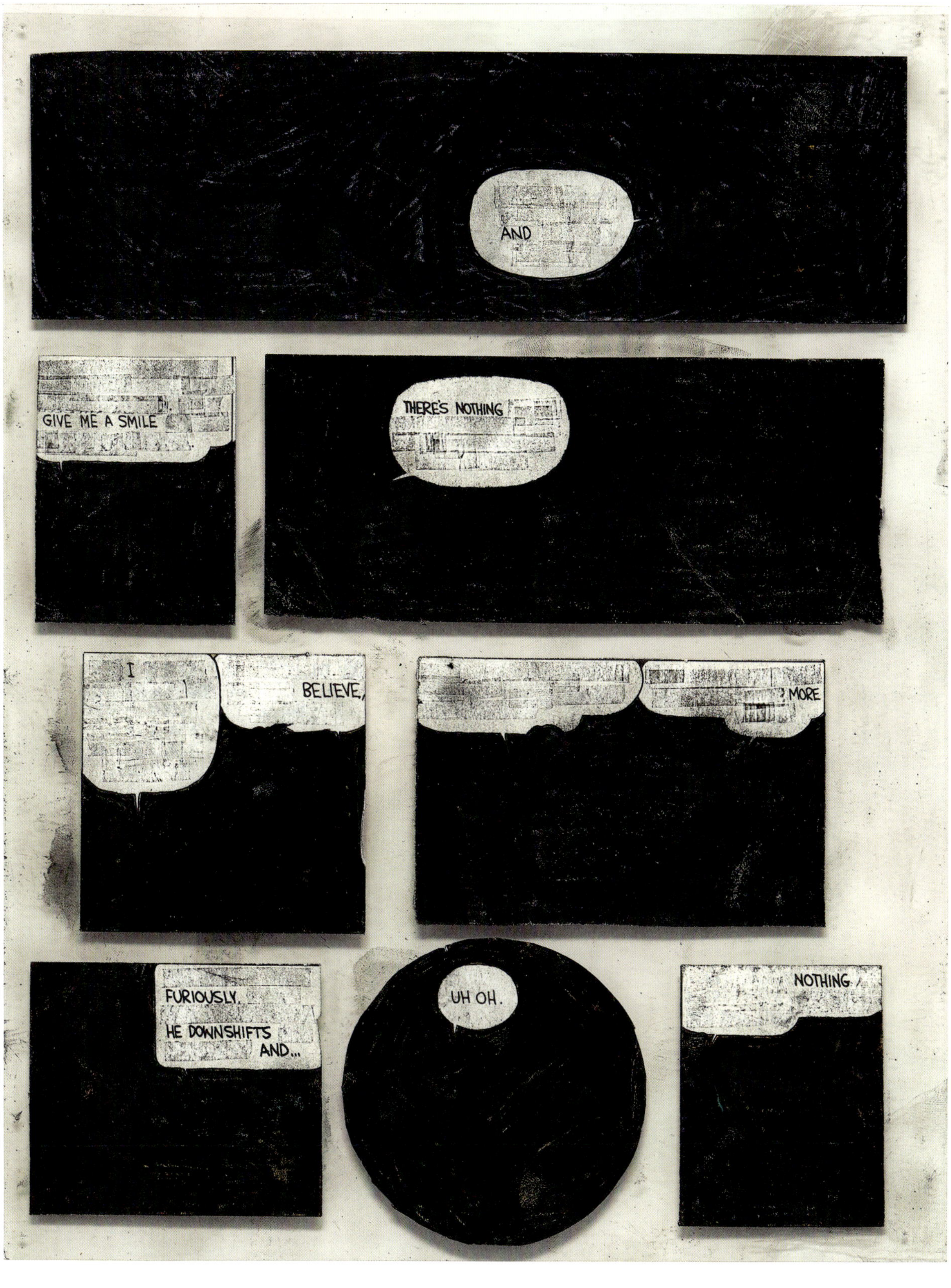
AND
GIVE ME A SMILE
THERE'S NOTHING
I
BELIEVE,
MORE
FURIOUSLY,
HE DOWNSHIFTS AND...
UH OH.
NOTHING.

Life Doubt

? Survive death
Doom!
I can't take
Myself!
You
Hope
You're making
Objects no longer diminish
Occasionally

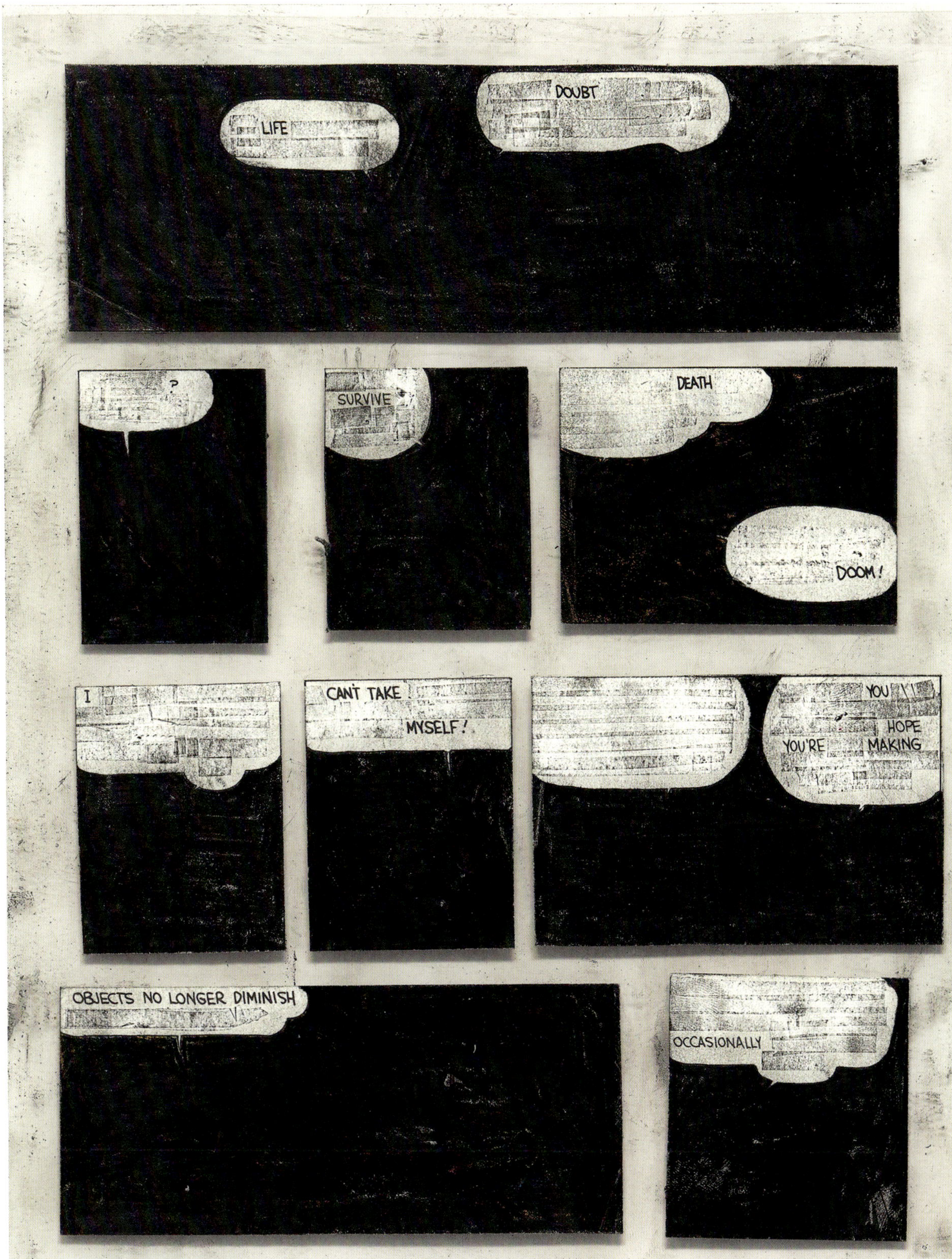
LIFE
DOUBT
?
SURVIVE
DEATH
DOOM!
I
CAN'T TAKE MYSELF!
YOU HOPE YOU'RE MAKING
OBJECTS NO LONGER DIMINISH
OCCASIONALLY

Better Than

Ready? The window is.
What trouble!
What I would be
Up,
                    A
     Million
. . . Three!

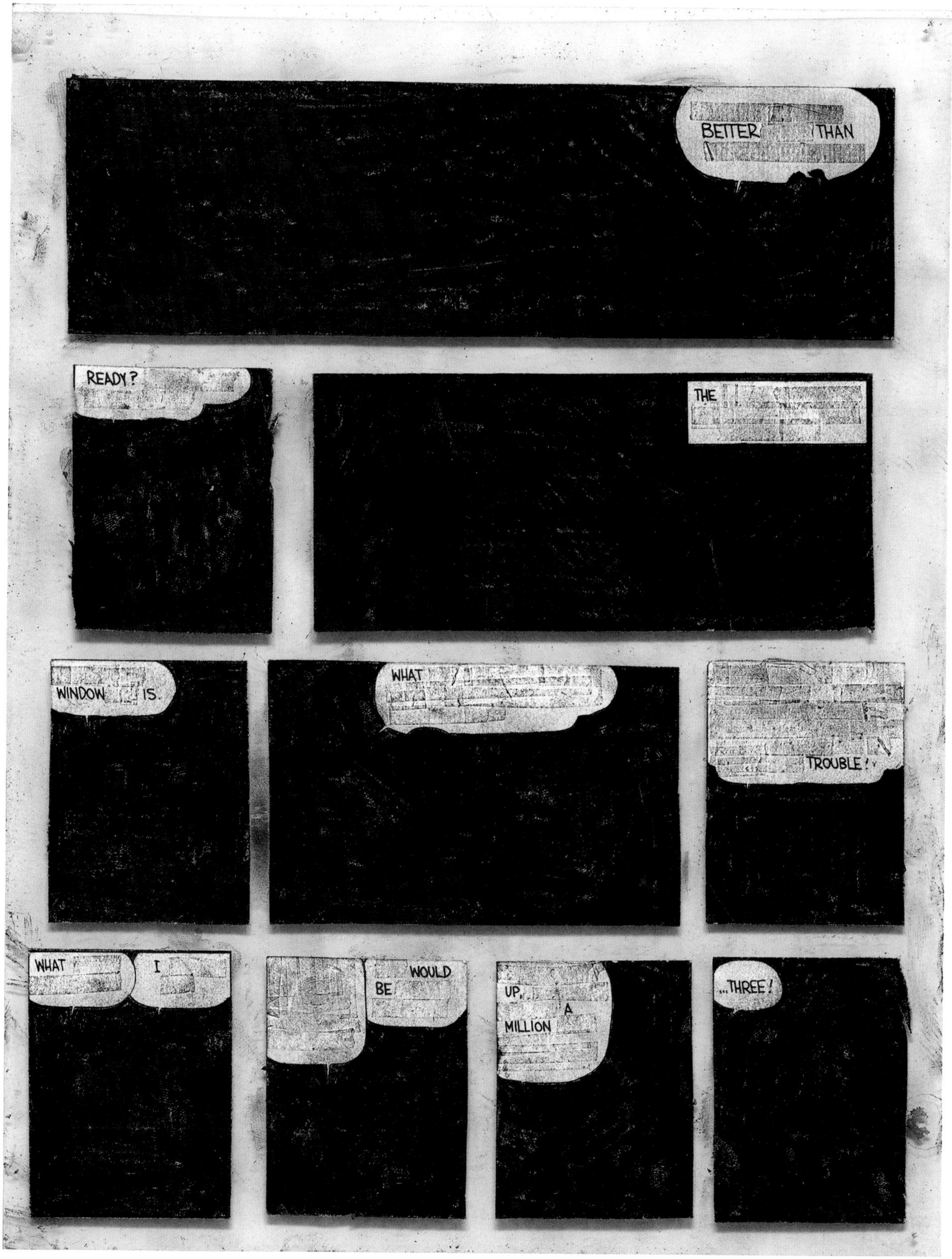

BETTER THAN
READY?
THE
WINDOW IS.
WHAT
TROUBLE!
WHAT I
WOULD BE
UP, A MILLION
...THREE!

Good Night,

Everything is
Muffled   These
Days,
                                        My
Childhood is forever. I hate
When it's not
    I should
Hear you
                        But I
Didn't know you

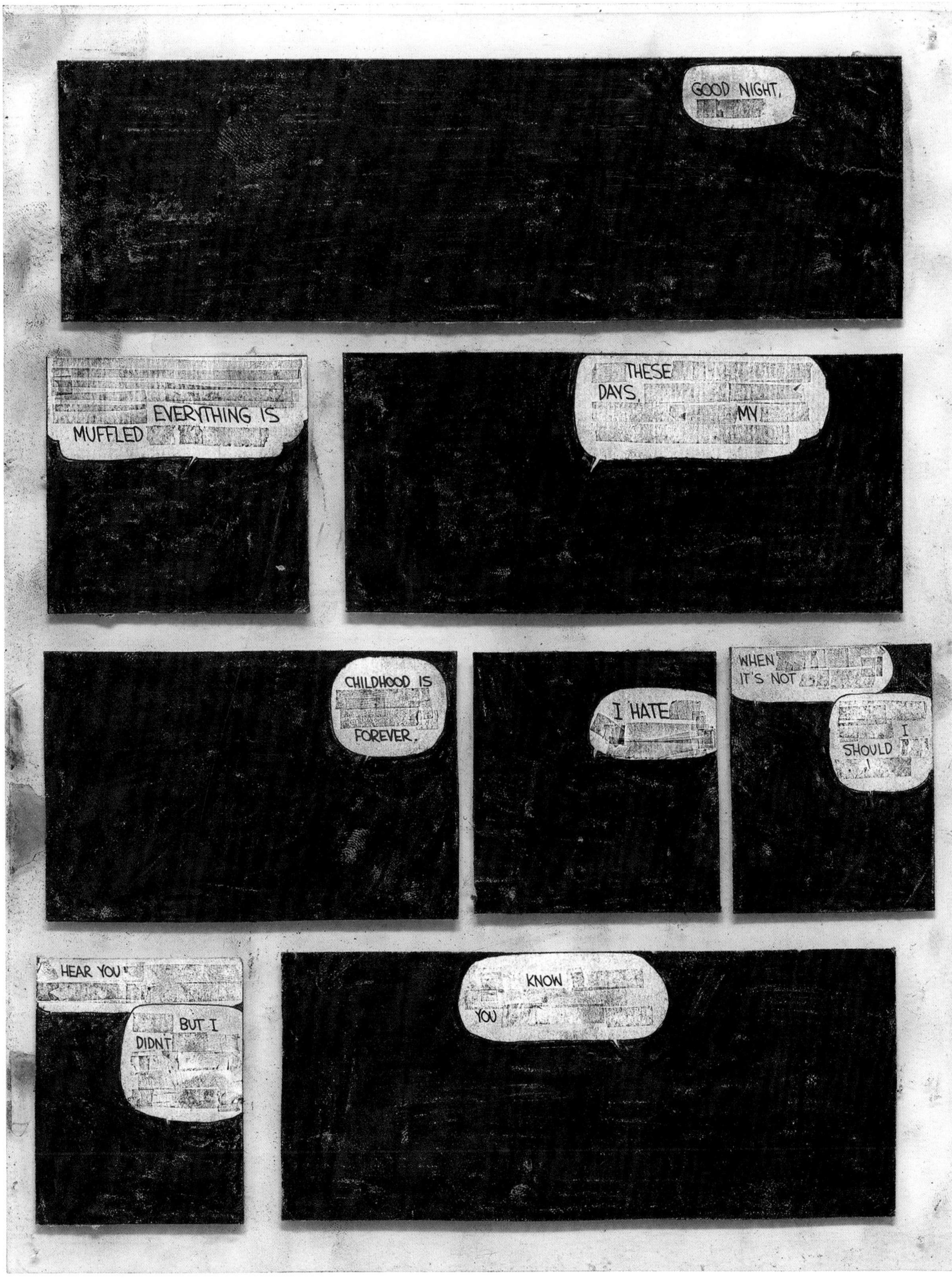
GOOD NIGHT,
EVERYTHING IS MUFFLED
THESE DAYS, MY
CHILDHOOD IS FOREVER.
I HATE
WHEN IT'S NOT
I SHOULD
HEAR YOU
BUT I DIDN'T
KNOW YOU

No Object

Don't just
Stand there,
            Help
Me
You take more!
                              Hurry
Maybe you can before the
Fall
Because it's raining.

We
Were working
While you wait
You couldn't   find
A face
Of
                    Another

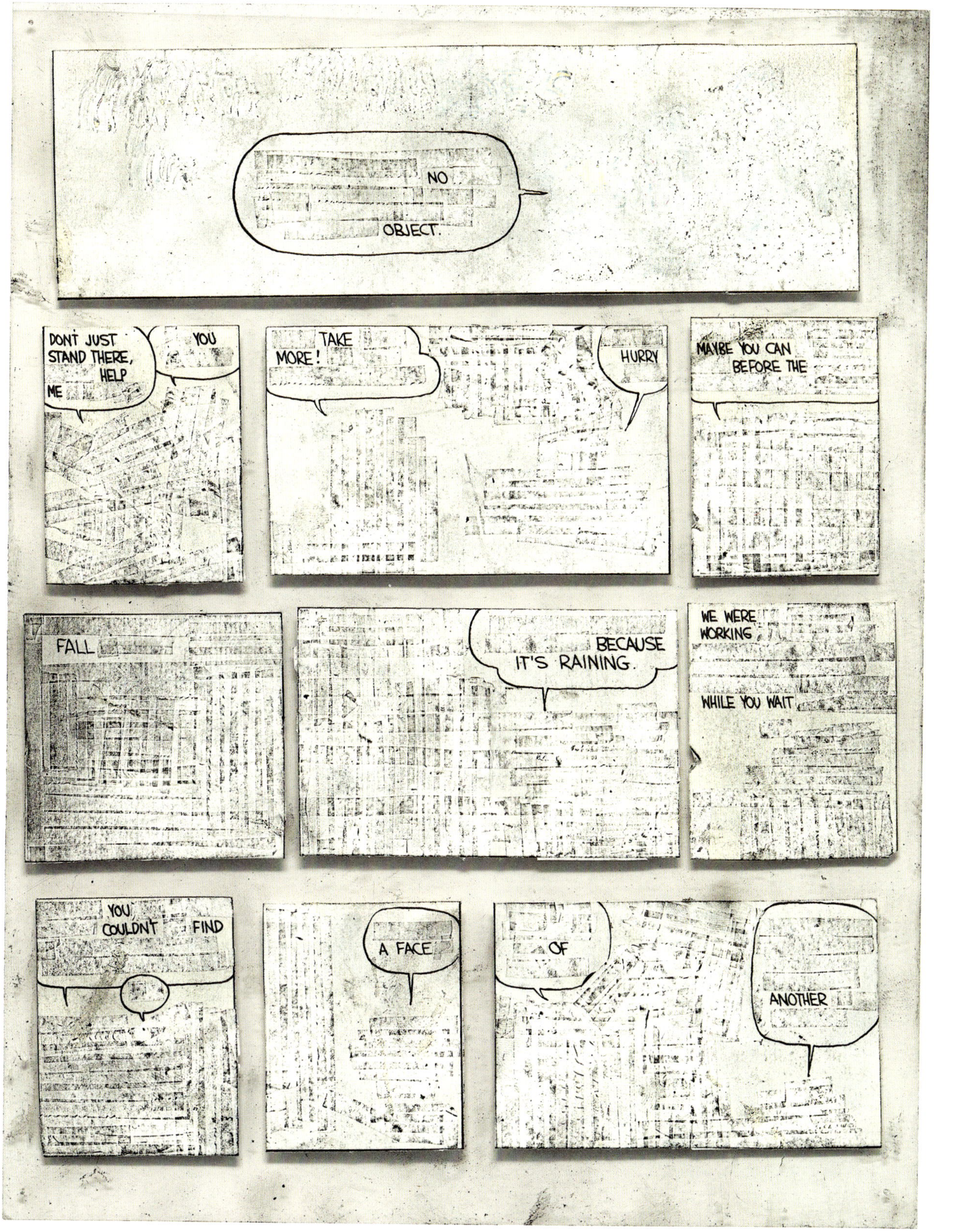
NO
OBJECT.
DON'T JUST STAND THERE, HELP ME
YOU
TAKE MORE!
HURRY
MAYBE YOU CAN BEFORE THE
FALL
BECAUSE IT'S RAINING.
WE WERE WORKING
WHILE YOU WAIT
YOU COULDN'T FIND
A FACE
OF
ANOTHER

Go

Go
There's nothing to
See!   It's
Ferocious
          And terrible
death!
Garbage.
  I should
Appreciate the
Slow
Kind

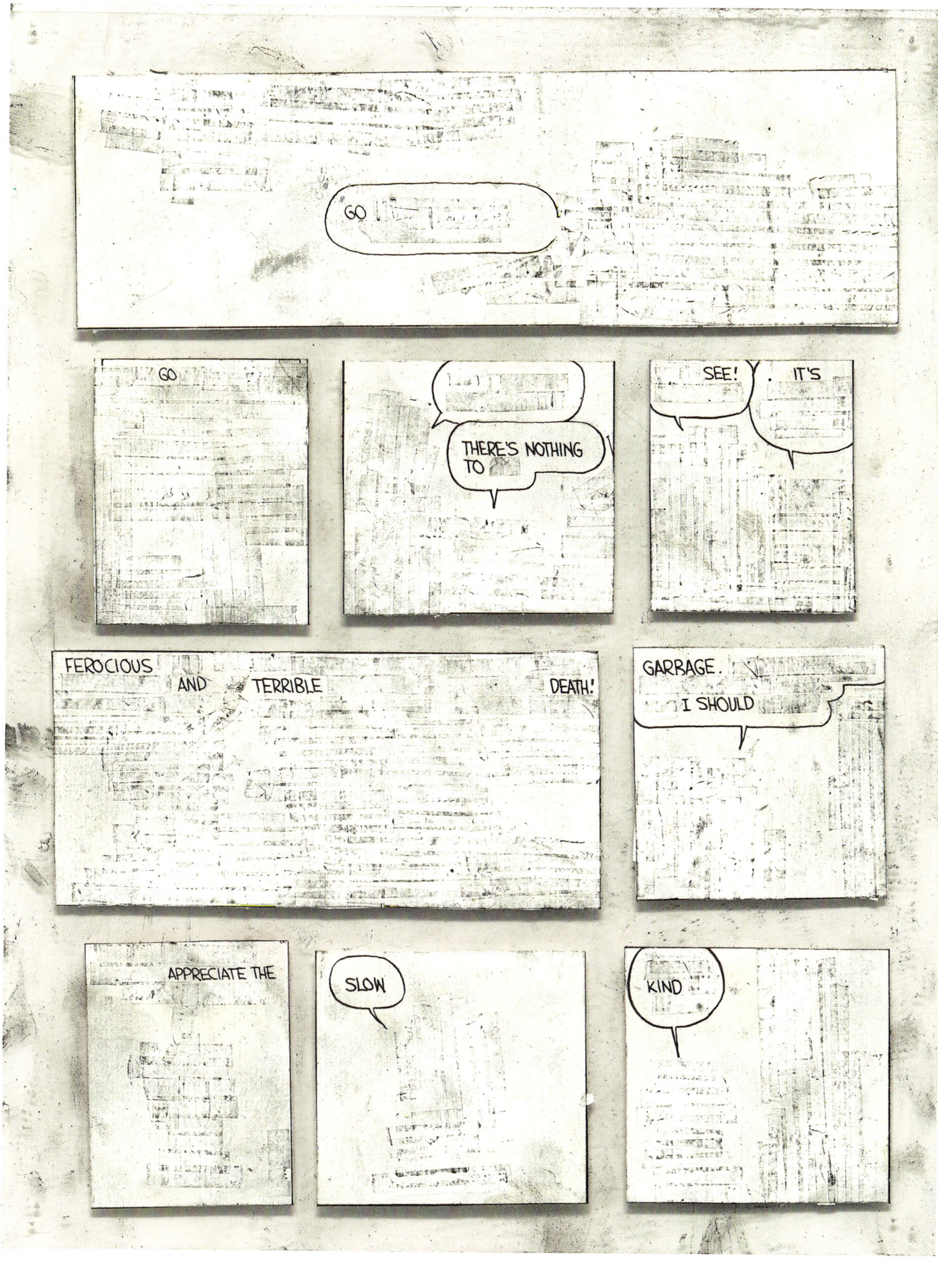
GO
GO
THERE'S NOTHING TO
SEE!
IT'S
FEROCIOUS
AND
TERRIBLE
DEATH!
GARBAGE.
I SHOULD
APPRECIATE THE
SLOW
KIND

Slaughterhouse

I think they make

This big on purpose.
And
Eat
    The tiger,
And . . .
        Red defeat.

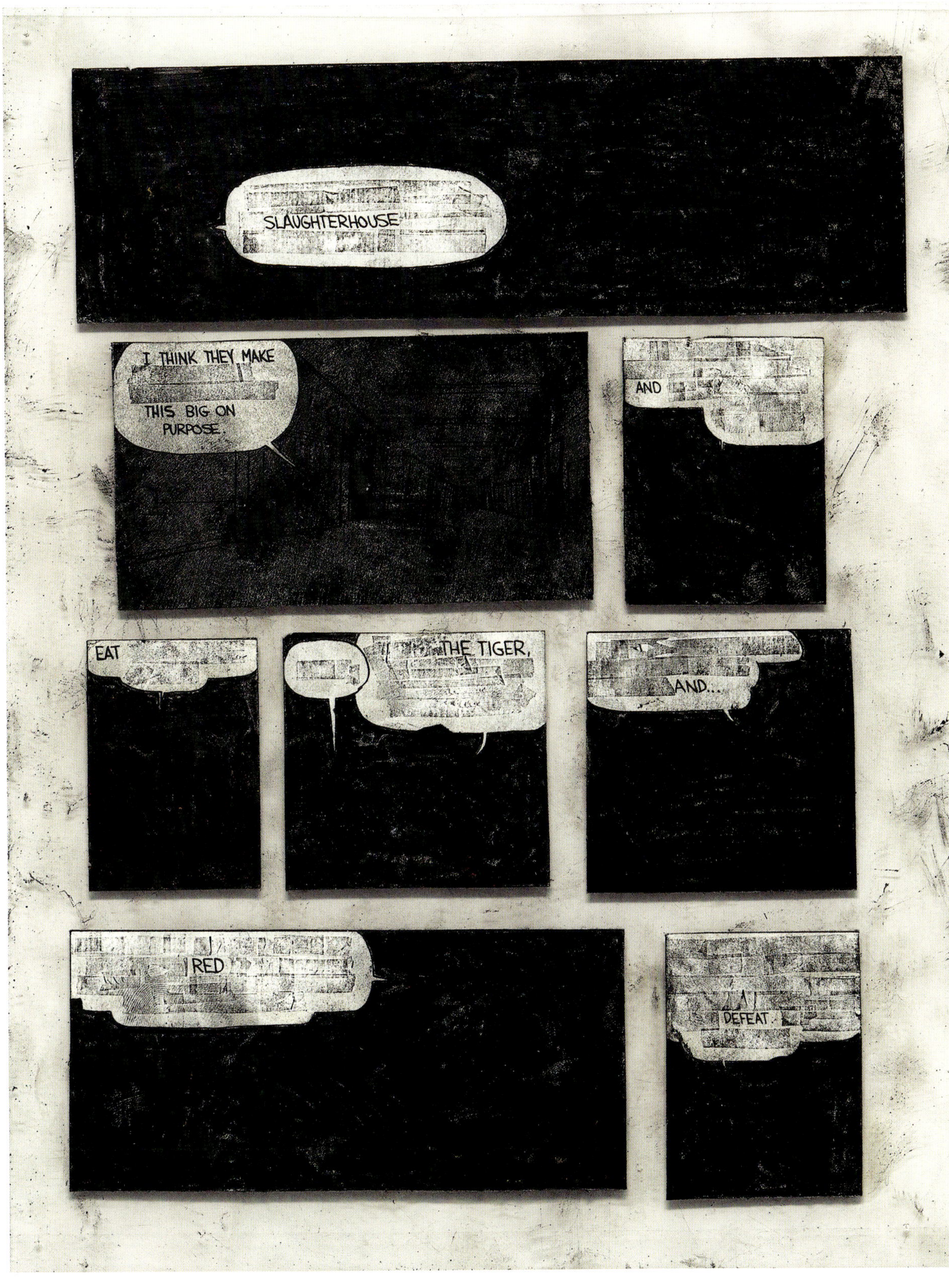
SLAUGHTERHOUSE
I THINK THEY MAKE
THIS BIG ON PURPOSE.
AND
EAT
THE TIGER,
AND...
RED
DEFEAT.

Tonight

Where have you
Been??
Nothing ever changes.
But
Everything
Was hopeless.
What
Do you
Have? Trapped
Time!
You can
Have
My
Dust

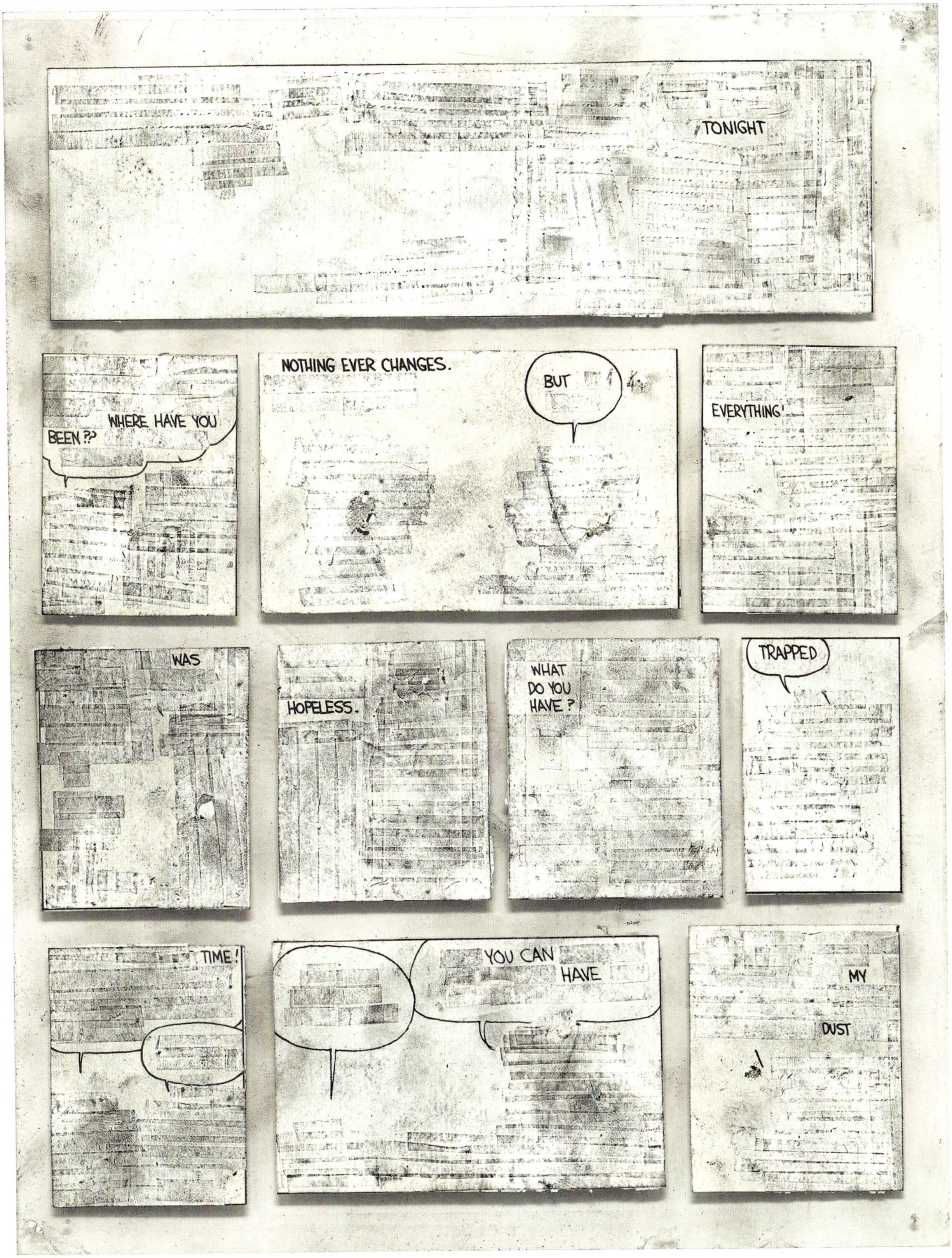
TONIGHT
WHERE HAVE YOU BEEN?!?
NOTHING EVER CHANGES.
BUT
EVERYTHING
WAS
HOPELESS.
WHAT DO YOU HAVE?
TRAPPED
TIME!
YOU CAN HAVE
MY
DUST

Too Far Apart

Both
Scared and
Wild
Wouldn't you say? No,
I came
Predestined
Into
Space!

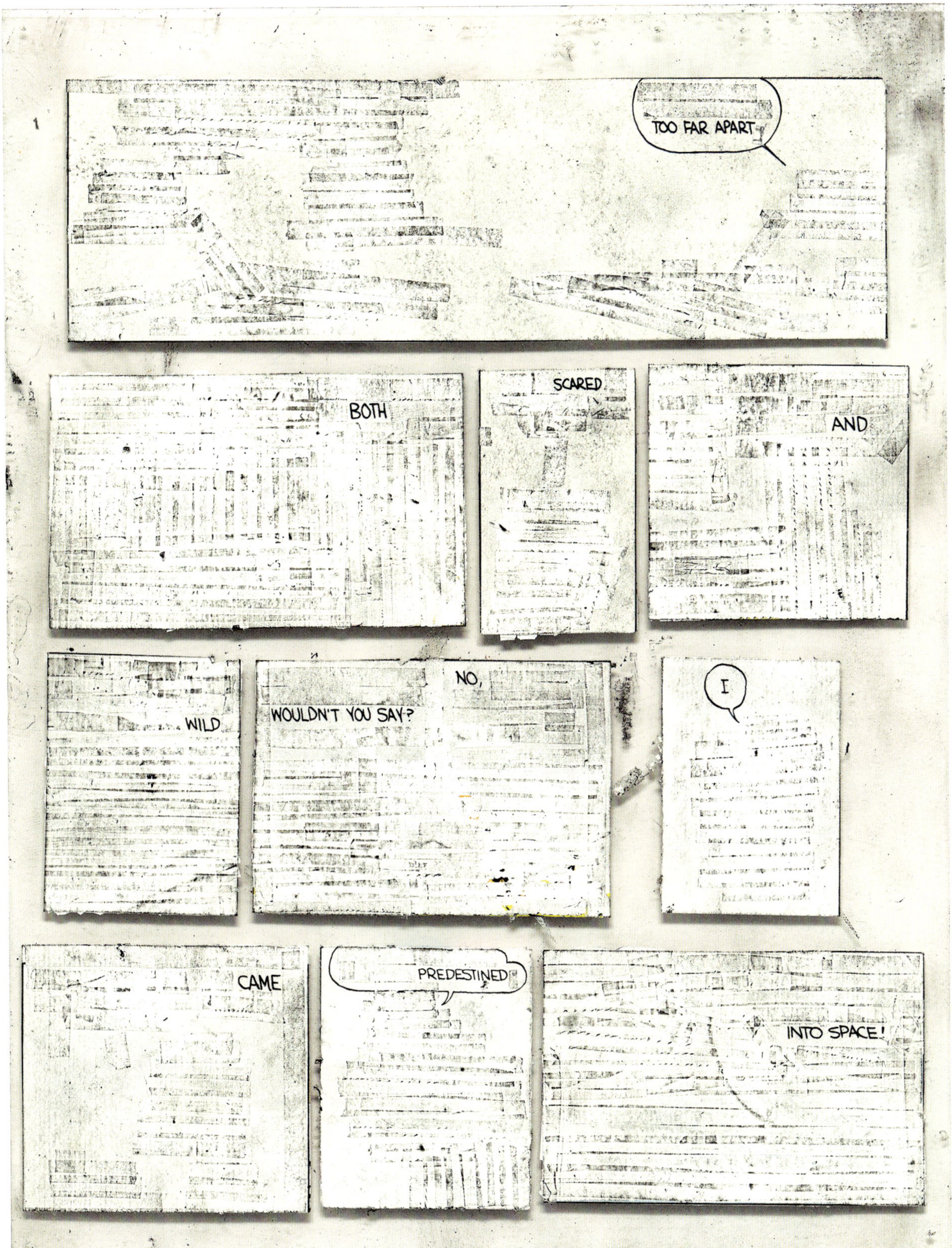

TOO FAR APART
BOTH
SCARED
AND
WILD
NO,
WOULDN'T YOU SAY?
I
CAME
PREDESTINED
INTO SPACE!

Around

Be the
Traitor
Pouring
the Torture
Believe but my
Motion! Or
Play time
I don't have

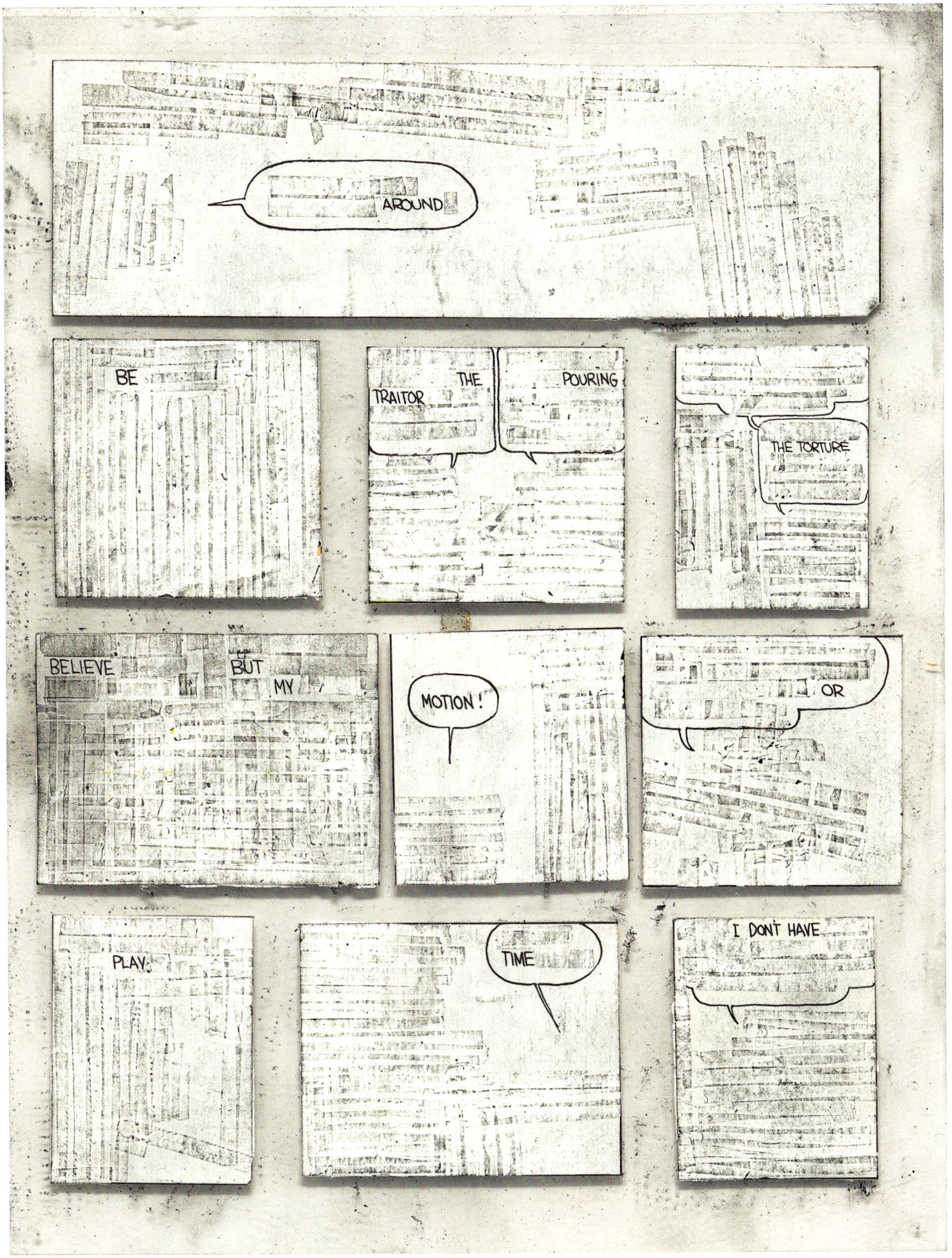

AROUND
BE
TRAITOR THE
POURING
THE TORTURE
BELIEVE
BUT
MY
MOTION!
OR
PLAY
TIME
I DON'T HAVE

The Opiate

Go then.
If you
Can
Outnumber
The inevitable.
A veritable defiance, We

Stand
With
A Captured
Attention
Span

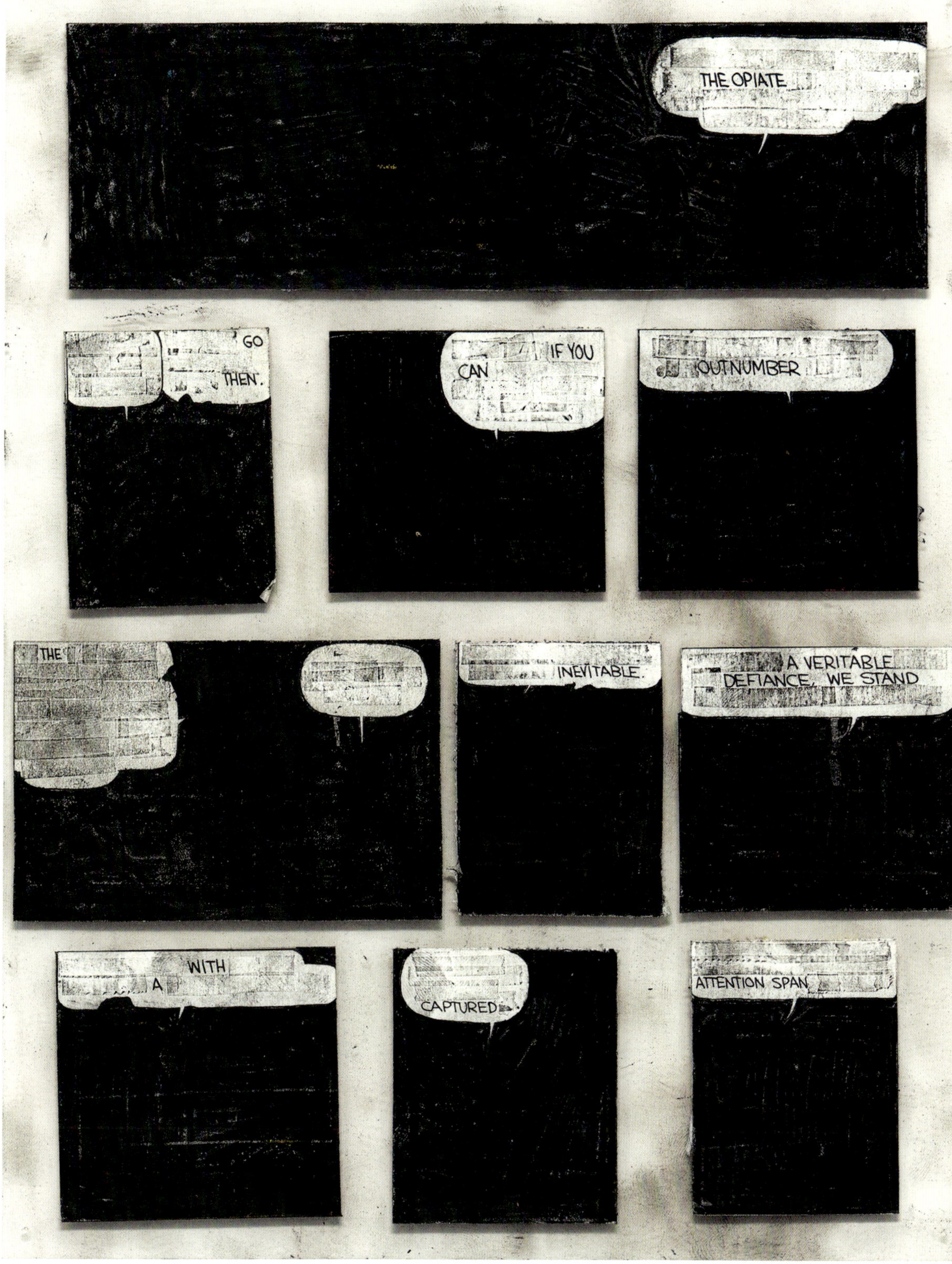
THE OPIATE
GO
THEN.
IF YOU
CAN
OUTNUMBER
THE
INEVITABLE.
A VERITABLE
DEFIANCE, WE STAND
WITH
A
CAPTURED
ATTENTION SPAN

glik glik glik

Death disintegrates
me.

High hope today,
I
Ask
Do you believe
In
Now?

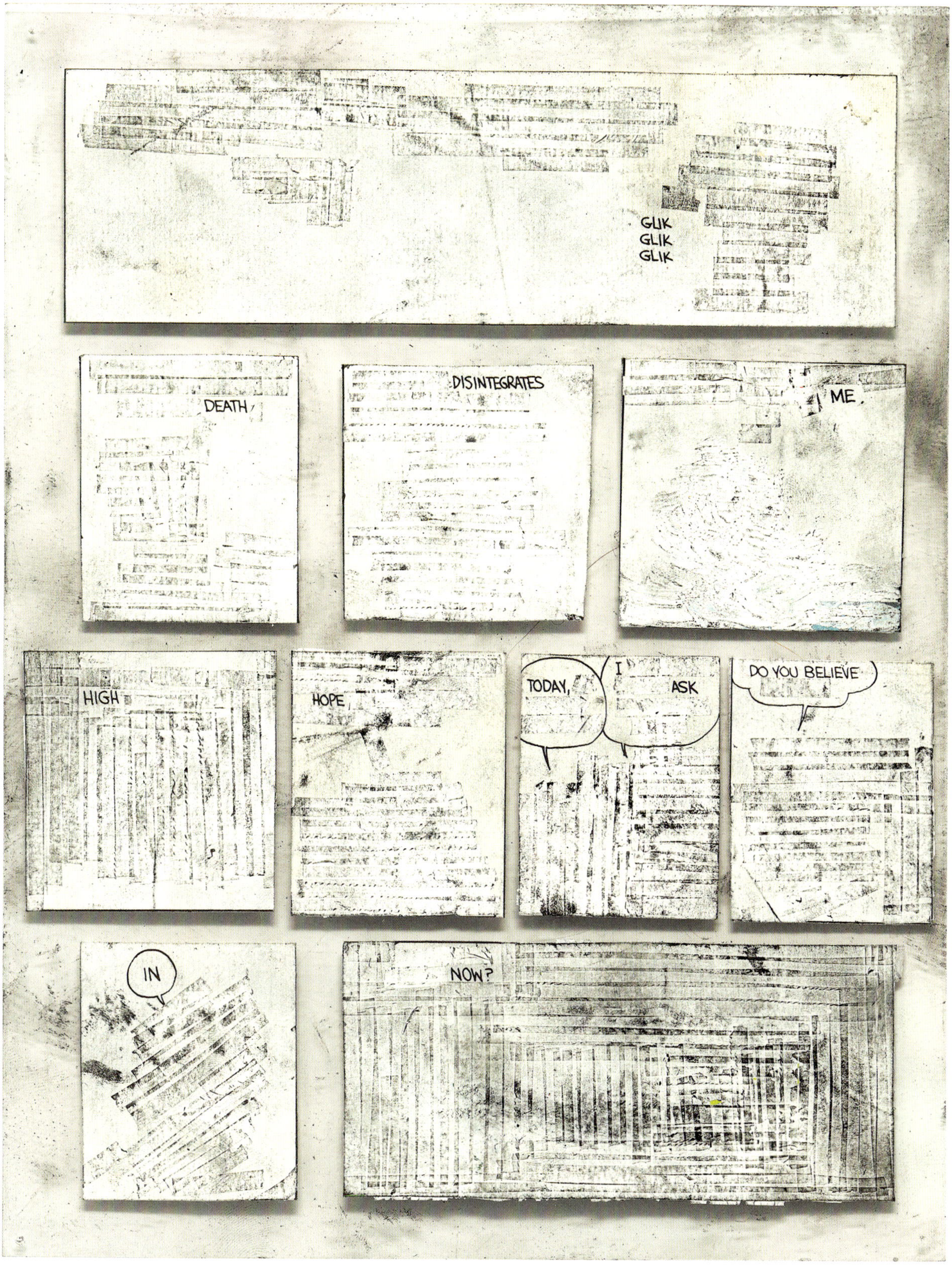
GLIK
GLIK
GLIK
DEATH
DISINTEGRATES
ME.
HIGH
HOPE
TODAY,
I
ASK
DO YOU BELIEVE
IN
NOW?

Our Fortress

Just imagine
At the slightest provocation,
you

Make it hard
Make her sing!
She
Squeals!
Always
Smells
Amazing
And you're still

Wet

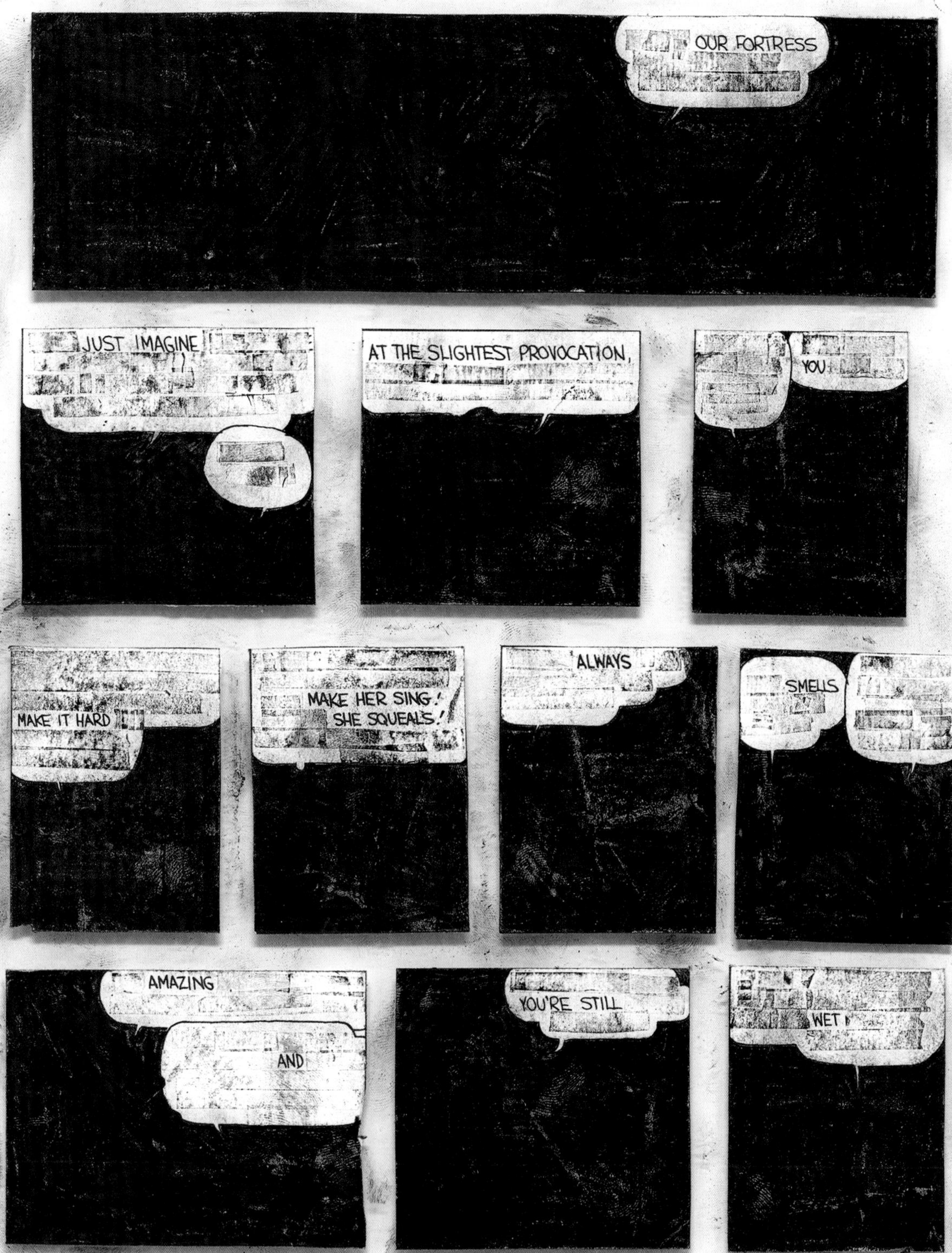
OUR FORTRESS
JUST IMAGINE
AT THE SLIGHTEST PROVOCATION,
YOU
MAKE IT HARD
MAKE HER SING!
SHE SQUEALS!
ALWAYS
SMELLS
AMAZING
AND
YOU'RE STILL
WET

Days

The beginning! I'm
Crashing through a face

That suggested a weird
Sense of humor, but I
Stopped
                    Moments before
So
Everyone can see now.
Look! Look!

And See

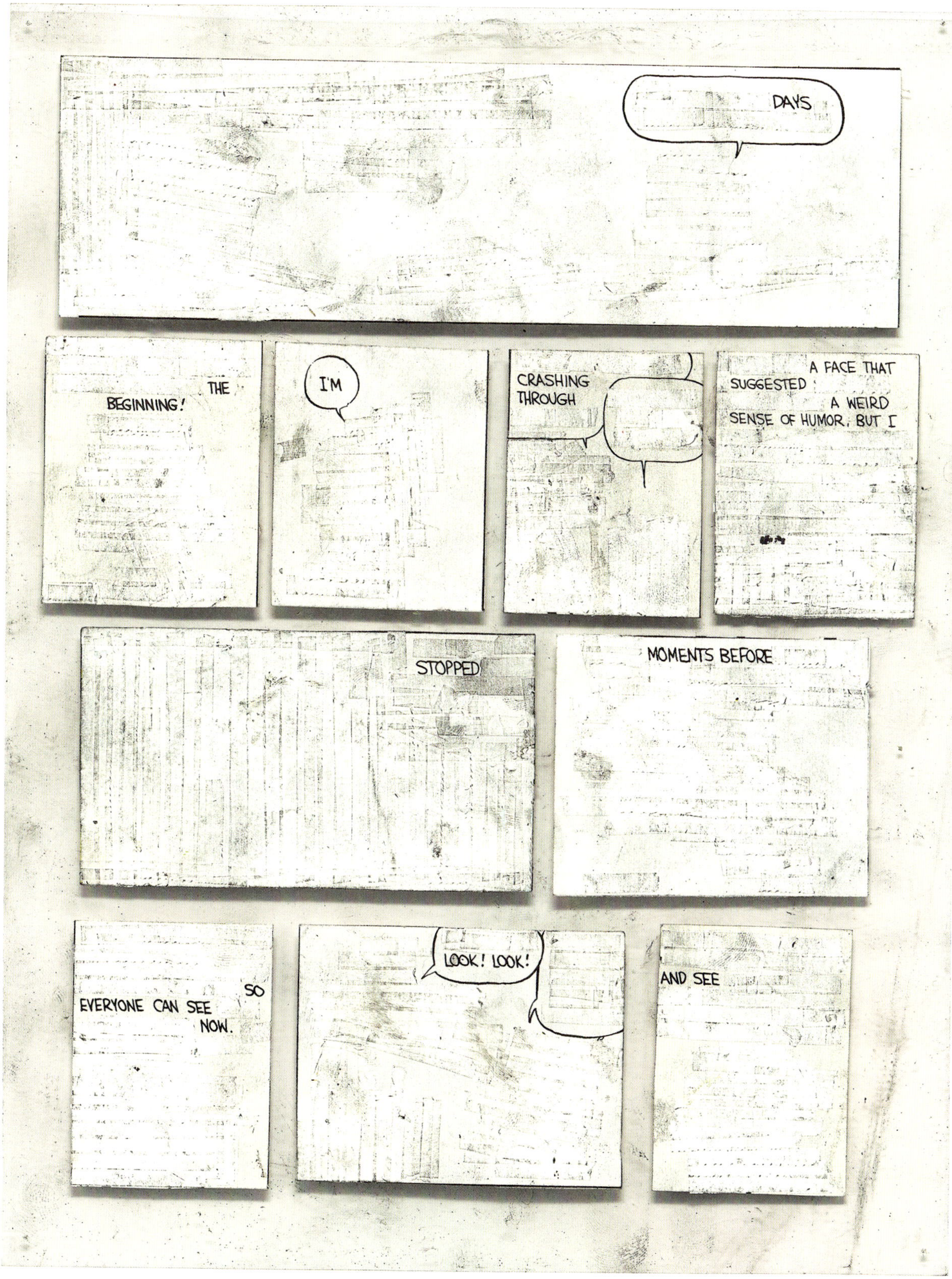
DAYS
THE BEGINNING!
I'M
CRASHING THROUGH
A FACE THAT SUGGESTED A WEIRD SENSE OF HUMOR, BUT I
STOPPED
MOMENTS BEFORE
SO EVERYONE CAN SEE NOW.
LOOK! LOOK!
AND SEE

Exit Next/Next Exit

Quit.
Right
Now.
What are you, a
Ferocious
Fearless
Desolate world of
Deep trouble?
What are you?
On the lam.

About time I get on the highway.

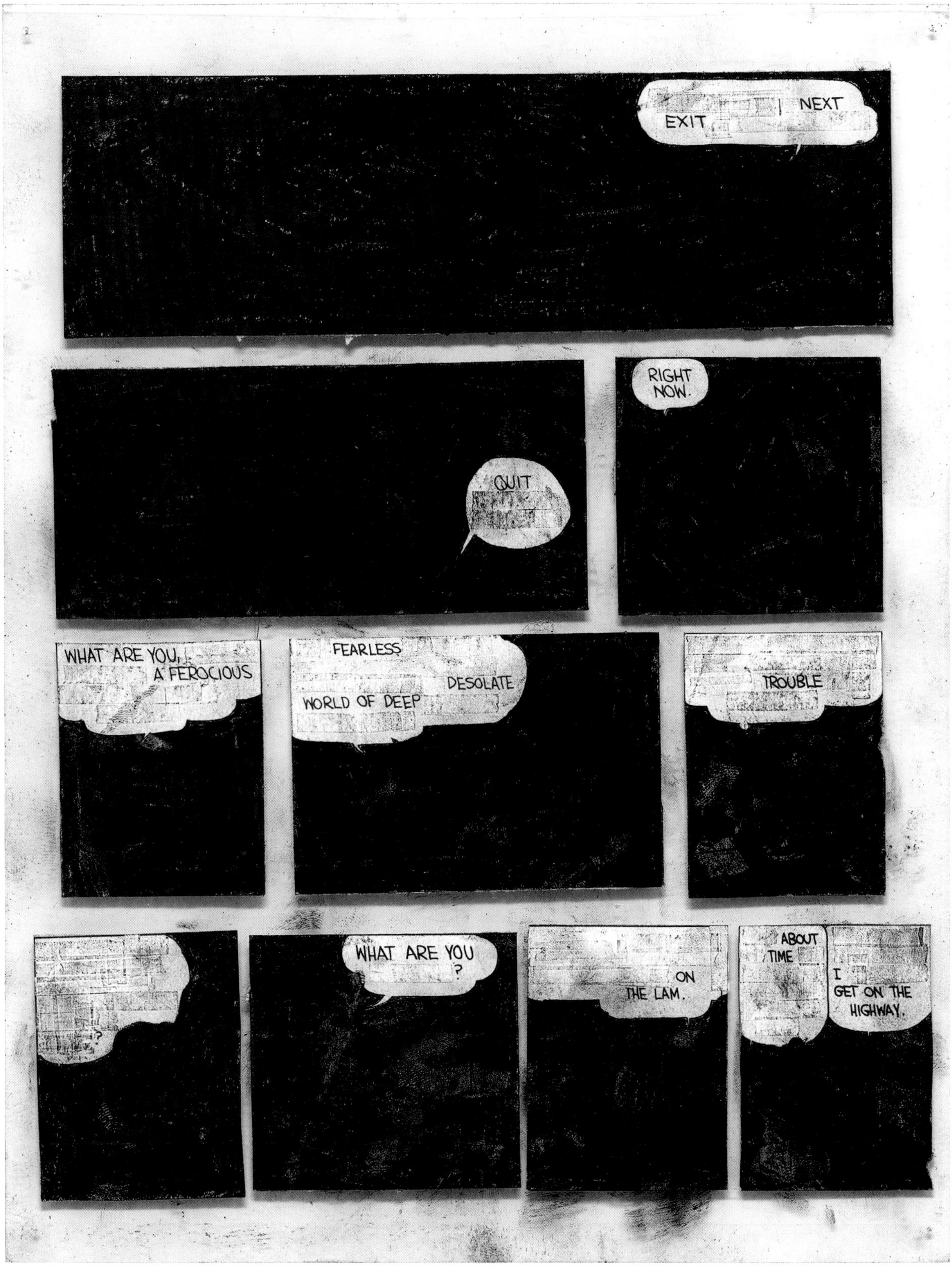
EXIT NEXT
QUIT
RIGHT NOW.
WHAT ARE YOU, A FEROCIOUS
FEARLESS DESOLATE WORLD OF DEEP
TROUBLE
?
WHAT ARE YOU ?
ON THE LAM.
ABOUT TIME
I GET ON THE HIGHWAY.

Maybe

The Blackness! Our

Bleeding wonder Our
Consciousness at the feet of
Sarcastic questions

I know the answers to I

Kiss the sweet ground!
                    Lifeless
world!
Maybe
          You should too.

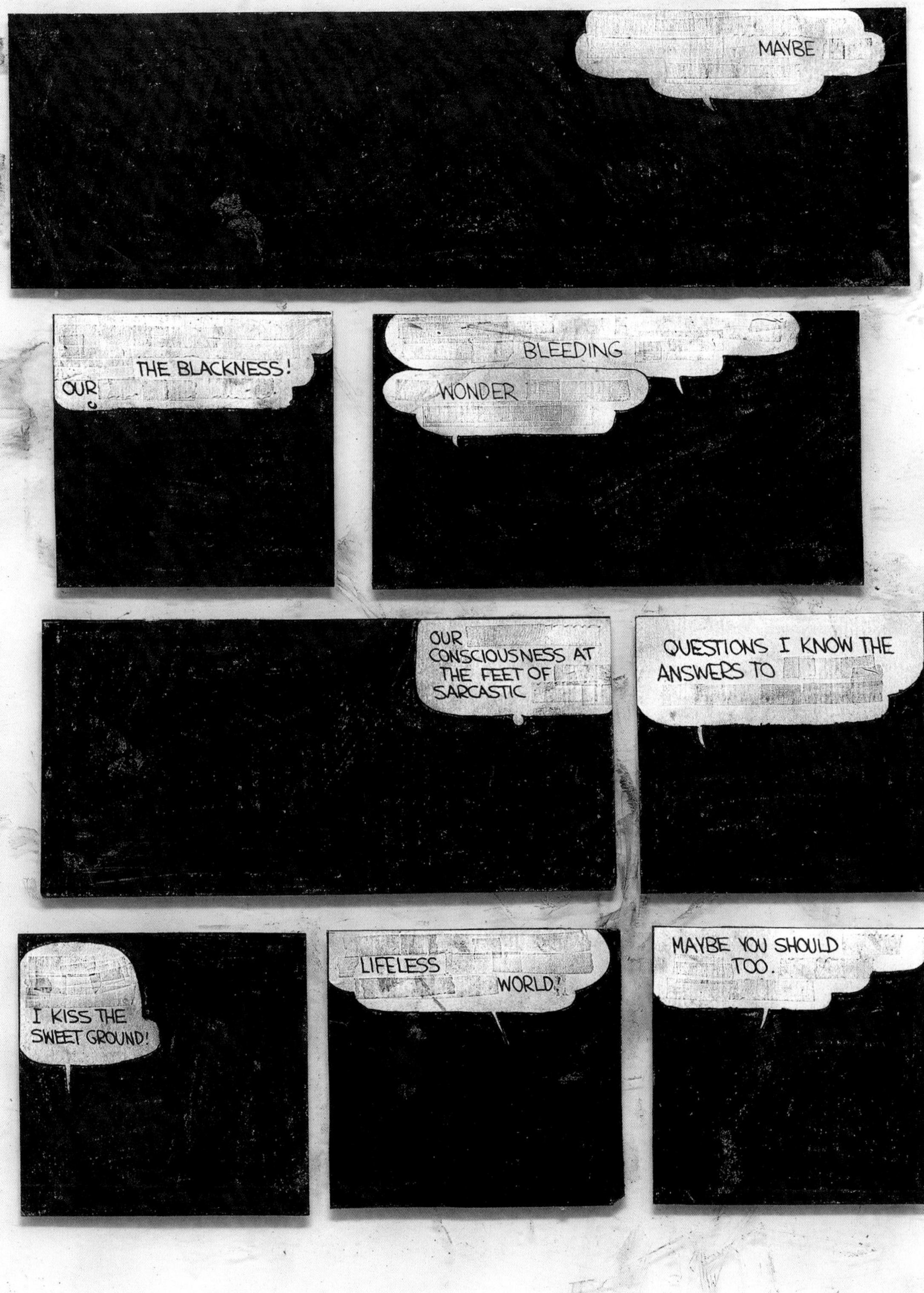
MAYBE
OUR THE BLACKNESS!
BLEEDING
WONDER
OUR CONSCIOUSNESS AT THE FEET OF SARCASTIC
QUESTIONS I KNOW THE ANSWERS TO
I KISS THE SWEET GROUND!
LIFELESS WORLD!
MAYBE YOU SHOULD TOO.

Good

Take one.
Hold
still. Drink. Again,
Power

And soft burns
This melts life.

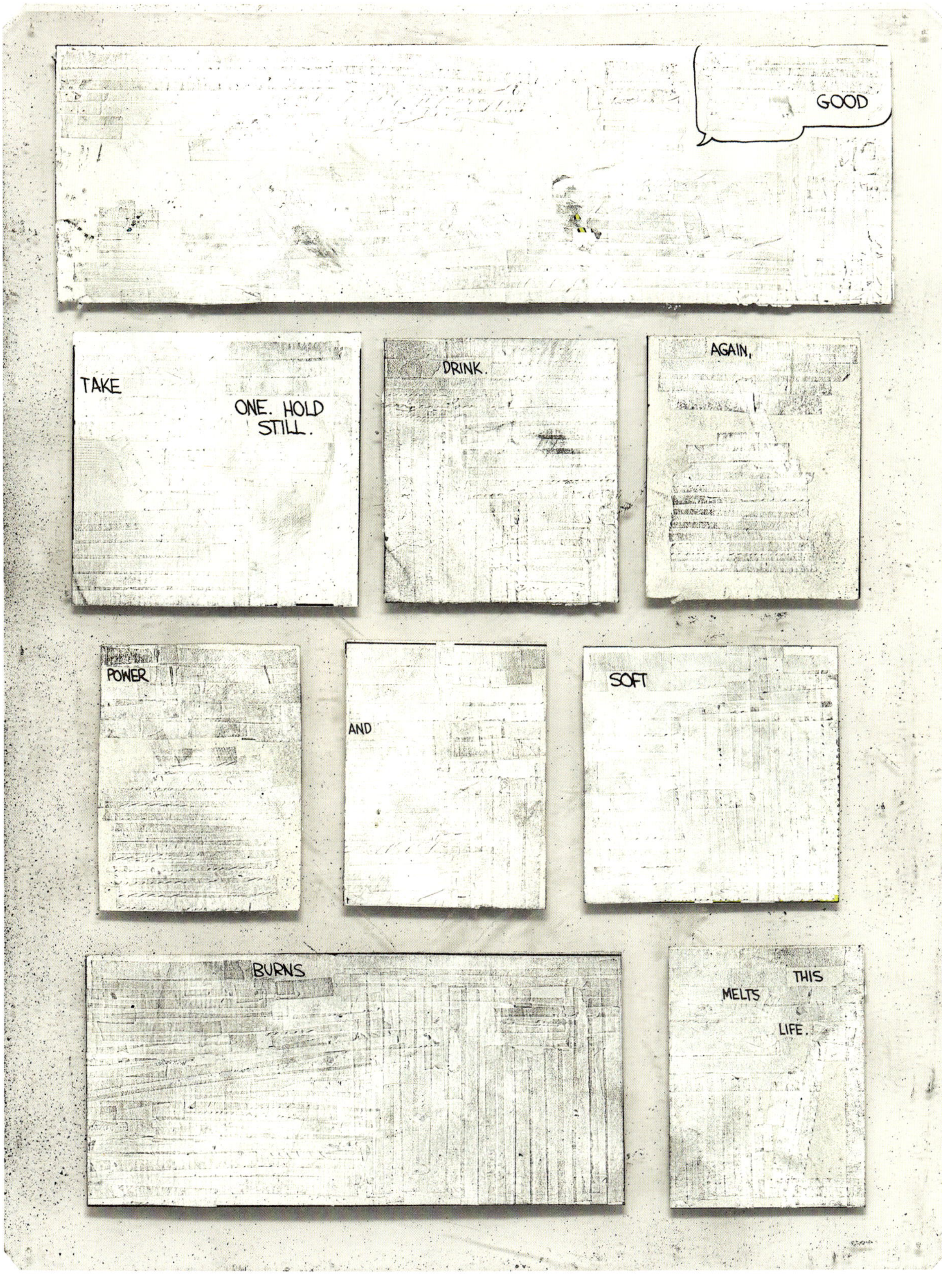
GOOD
TAKE
ONE. HOLD STILL.
DRINK.
AGAIN,
POWER
AND
SOFT
BURNS
MELTS
THIS
LIFE.

The She

Do I have to   know

                    Myself

? Not for a
Long time. That's good.

I have to get up

And just

Look, see, and

Squeeze through this

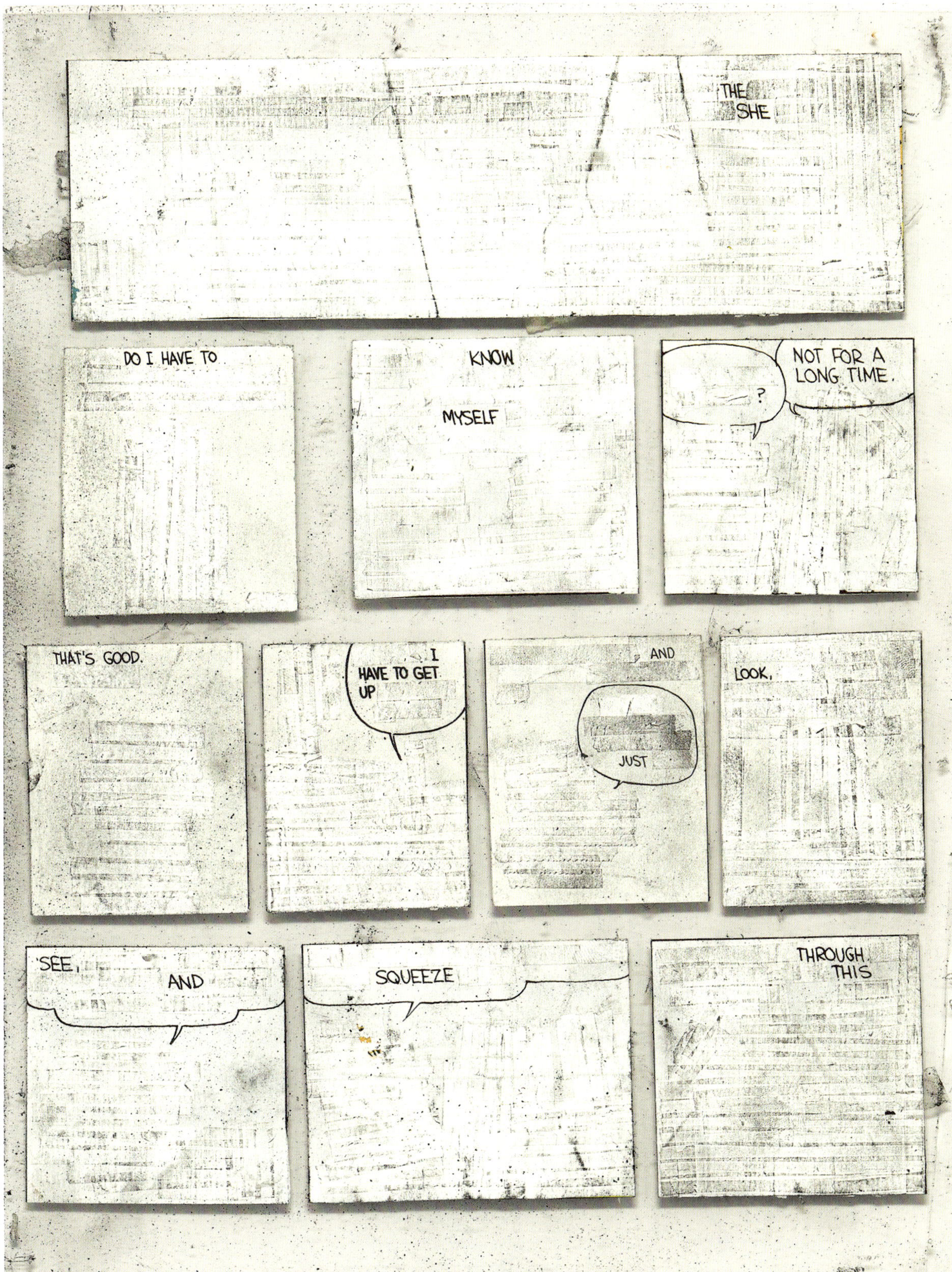
THE
SHE
DO I HAVE TO
KNOW
MYSELF
?
NOT FOR A LONG TIME.
THAT'S GOOD.
I HAVE TO GET UP
AND
JUST
LOOK,
SEE,
AND
SQUEEZE
THROUGH THIS

Ready

I don't know.
I don't think I'm
Gonna make it.

I'm trying to join our
struggles and

I was afraid you wouldn't
believe me.
What if I was me?? What's
going on,

I wonder.

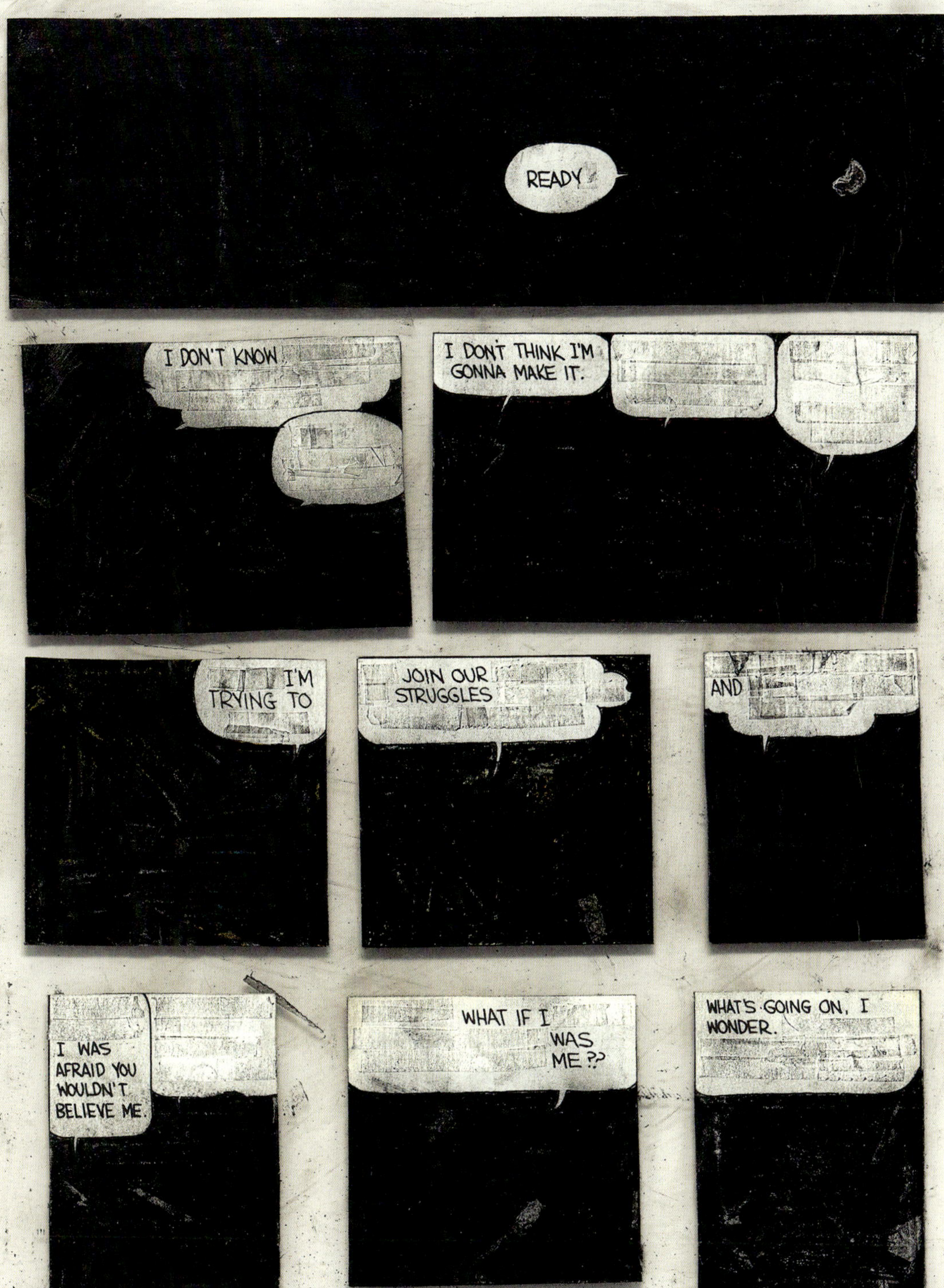
READY
I DON'T KNOW
I DON'T THINK I'M GONNA MAKE IT.
I'M TRYING TO
JOIN OUR STRUGGLES
AND
I WAS AFRAID YOU WOULDN'T BELIEVE ME.
WHAT IF I WAS ME ?!?
WHAT'S GOING ON, I WONDER.

Father

What are you doing?
          The baby
     Is here!
Be good

Philistine genius of better
education I always wanted

Let's go outside and
Make
     Tomorrow
     Things.

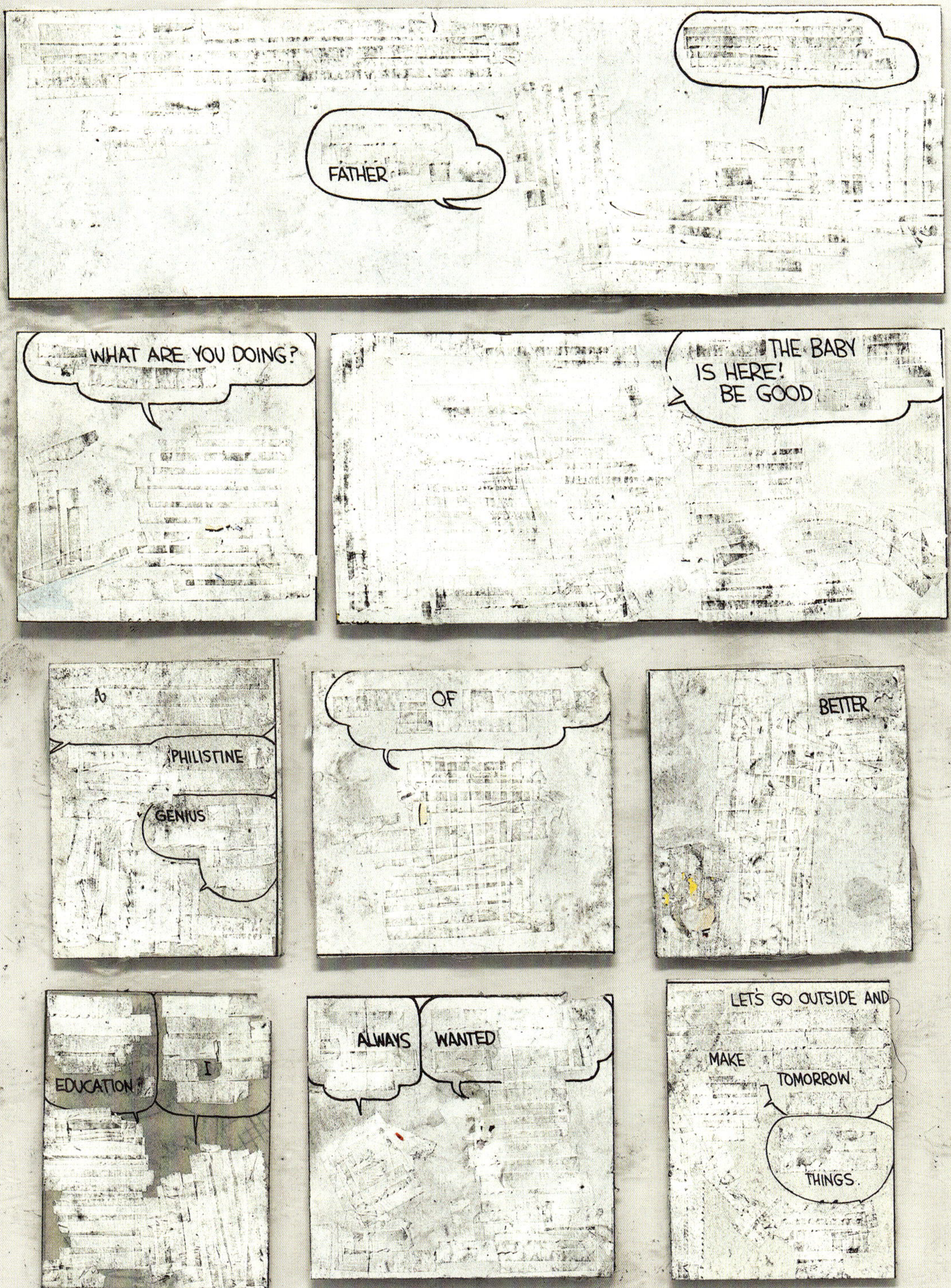
FATHER
WHAT ARE YOU DOING?
THE BABY IS HERE! BE GOOD
A
PHILISTINE
GENIUS
OF
BETTER
EDUCATION
I
ALWAYS
WANTED
LET'S GO OUTSIDE AND
MAKE
TOMORROW.
THINGS.

The Beach

Refresh my memory.
                                        My
wine
A
Cigarette?   Cool.

You've made enough
Trips to the water already

If we imagined
                        We could
pretend it's not unlike
Here!

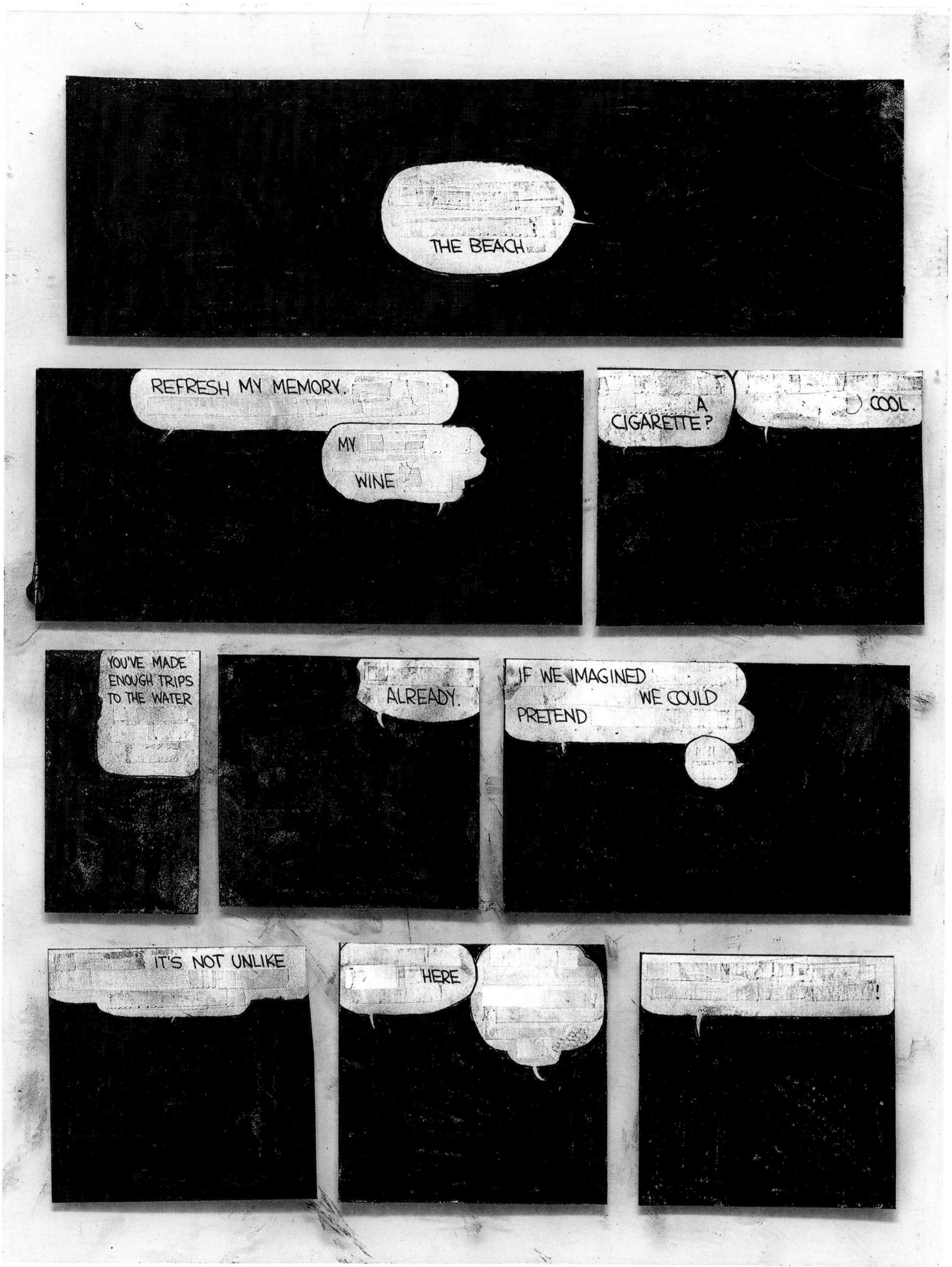
THE BEACH
REFRESH MY MEMORY.
MY WINE
A CIGARETTE?
COOL.
YOU'VE MADE ENOUGH TRIPS TO THE WATER
ALREADY.
IF WE IMAGINED WE COULD PRETEND
IT'S NOT UNLIKE
HERE
!

What

What the
Why   with

Wonder what

For . . . so what
of
You

Without why is we

The was

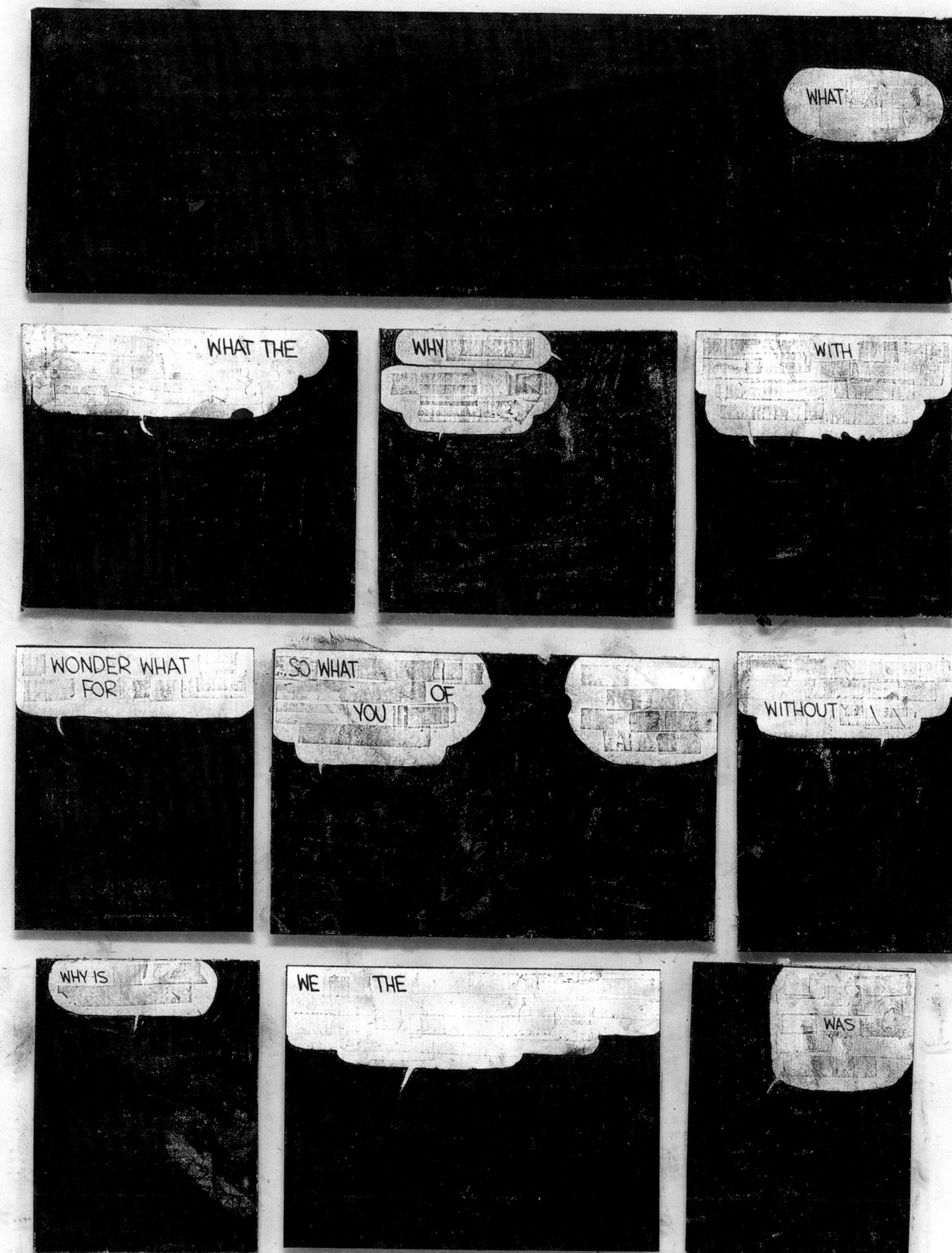
WHAT
WHAT THE
WHY
WITH
WONDER WHAT
FOR
SO WHAT
OF
YOU
WITHOUT
WHY IS
WE THE
WAS

The Planet

Hope don't come in boxes.
Dangerous and stupid.

Hypothetically, let's
Say
Hypothetically.
Hypothetically,
Man Lasts forever!

I'll
Sit still so
The bleeding
Can stop

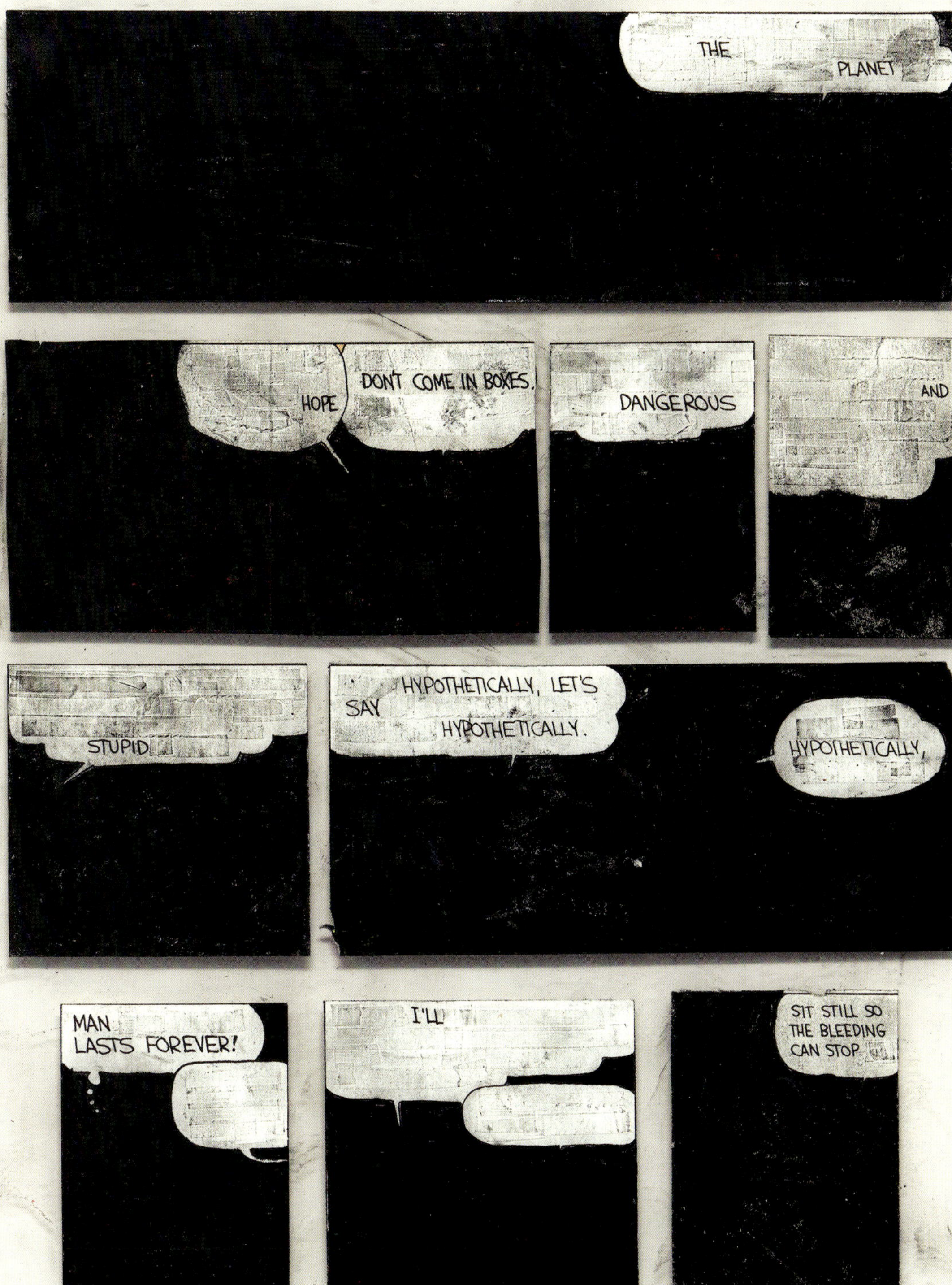
THE PLANET
HOPE
DON'T COME IN BOXES.
DANGEROUS
AND
STUPID
SAY HYPOTHETICALLY, LET'S HYPOTHETICALLY.
HYPOTHETICALLY,
MAN LASTS FOREVER!
I'LL
SIT STILL SO THE BLEEDING CAN STOP

If

If you
Go
thanks for the
... The peculiar ...
Peculiar
smell

And quiet

Nobody I

Was fighting for

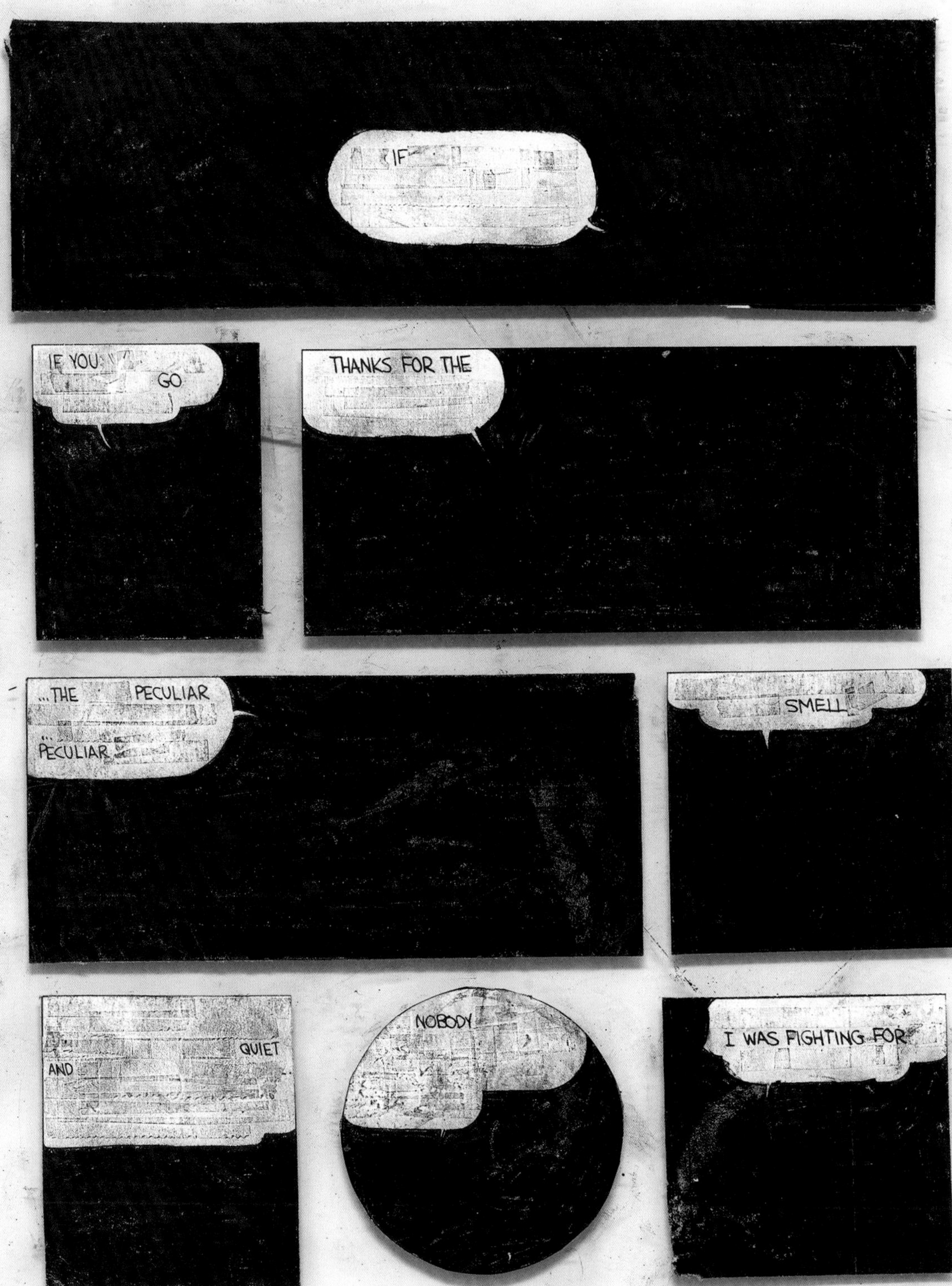
IF
IF YOU GO
THANKS FOR THE
...THE PECULIAR ...PECULIAR
SMELL
QUIET AND
NOBODY
I WAS FIGHTING FOR

Are You Nervous?

I don't hear
Anything.   Yet.

Why do these "walks" always end

Oh, the
            The way maybe
                        Is weakening.
you
Need to stay
You   and I'll pit wits

Against something

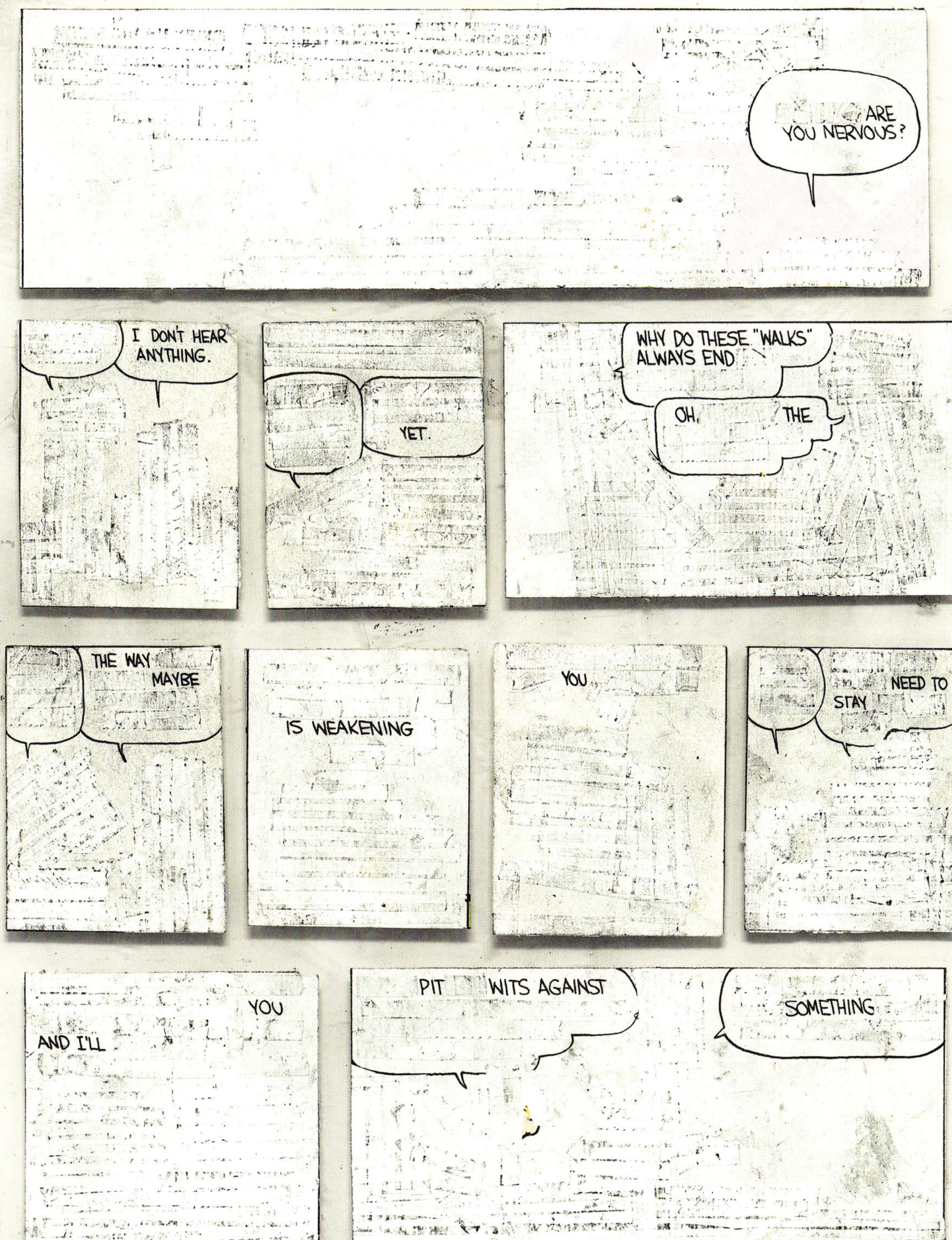
ARE YOU NERVOUS?
I DON'T HEAR ANYTHING.
YET.
WHY DO THESE "WALKS" ALWAYS END
OH, THE
THE WAY
MAYBE
IS WEAKENING
YOU
NEED TO
STAY
AND I'LL
YOU
PIT WITS AGAINST
SOMETHING

Untitled

I was
Blamed
For everything. You're not

Dumb dropping off torches? This

You Little Thug! You threaten
And acted Smug and
the

Question is,

. . . Why? Today I am living

Exploding more!

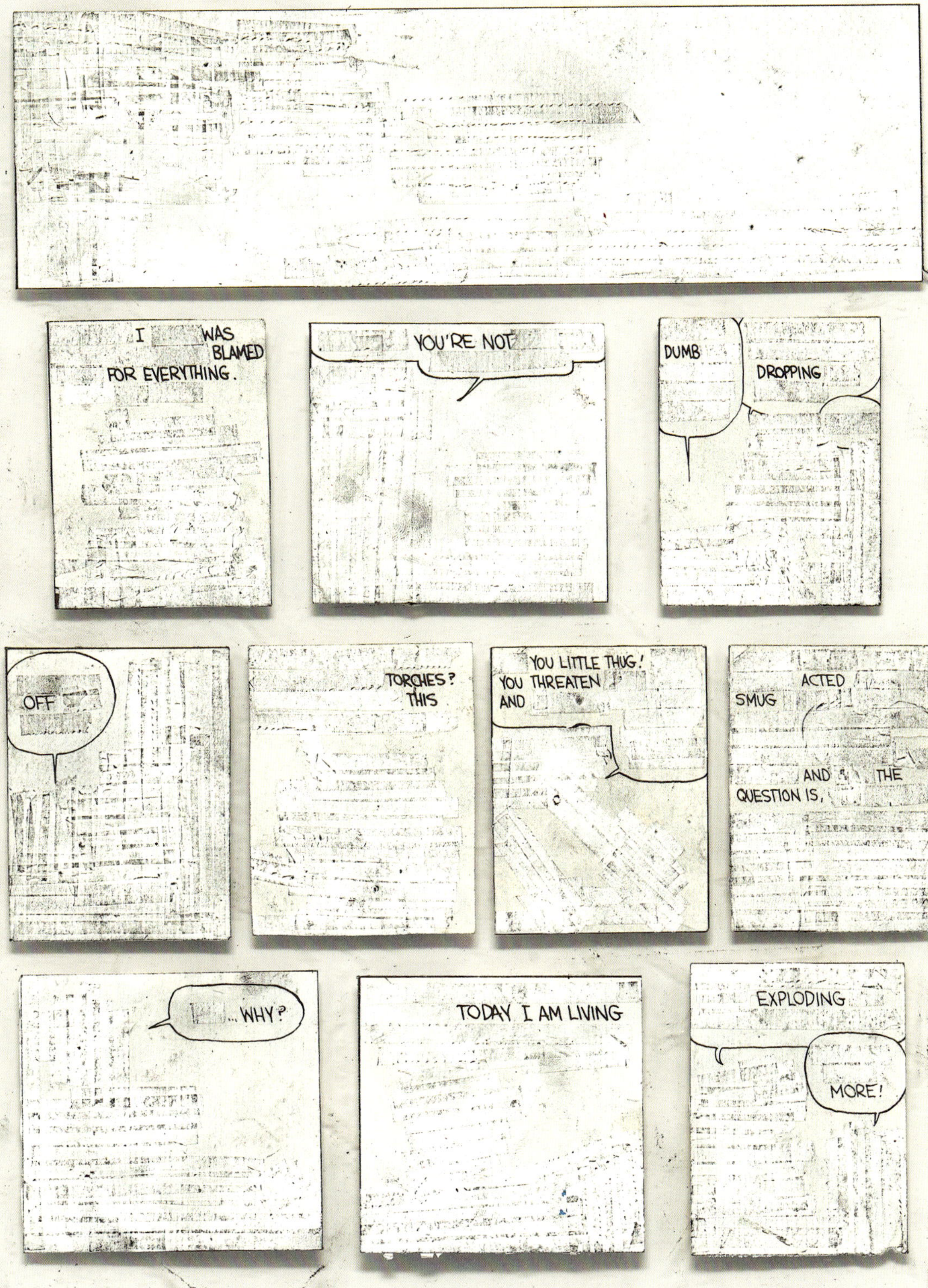
I WAS BLAMED FOR EVERYTHING.
YOU'RE NOT
DUMB
DROPPING
OFF
TORCHES? THIS
YOU LITTLE THUG! YOU THREATEN AND
SMUG ACTED
AND THE QUESTION IS,
...WHY?
TODAY I AM LIVING
EXPLODING
MORE!

The Monsters Monsters

Did you hear something?? There's no
                                        Answer.   Quiet.
Ugh. Something is Drooling.
The hungry attack us.

Thrashing about in a desperate
Bid for freedom, he only becomes
More entangled!
                        Well then, just sit
Here until we die.

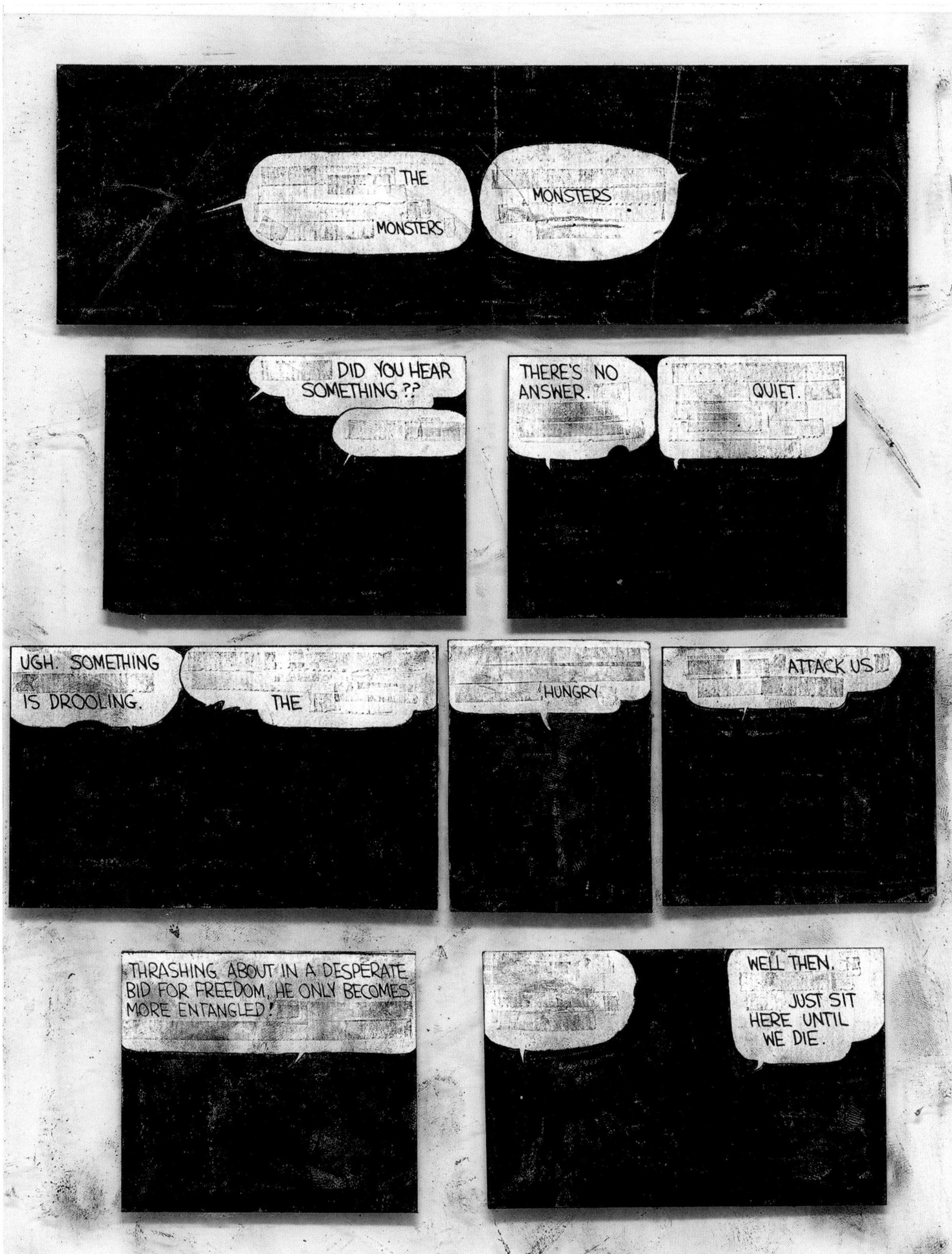
THE MONSTERS
MONSTERS
DID YOU HEAR SOMETHING ??
THERE'S NO ANSWER.
QUIET.
UGH. SOMETHING IS DROOLING.
THE
HUNGRY
ATTACK US
THRASHING ABOUT IN A DESPERATE BID FOR FREEDOM, HE ONLY BECOMES MORE ENTANGLED!
WELL THEN, JUST SIT HERE UNTIL WE DIE.

Should I or Shouldn't I?

This is our World a
generation that doesn't
Know anything
Look! Look,
You should see me
. . . Not that they do anyway . . .

It's too late to change your
mind

You
Make me
Hate you!
I can't stop stupid you

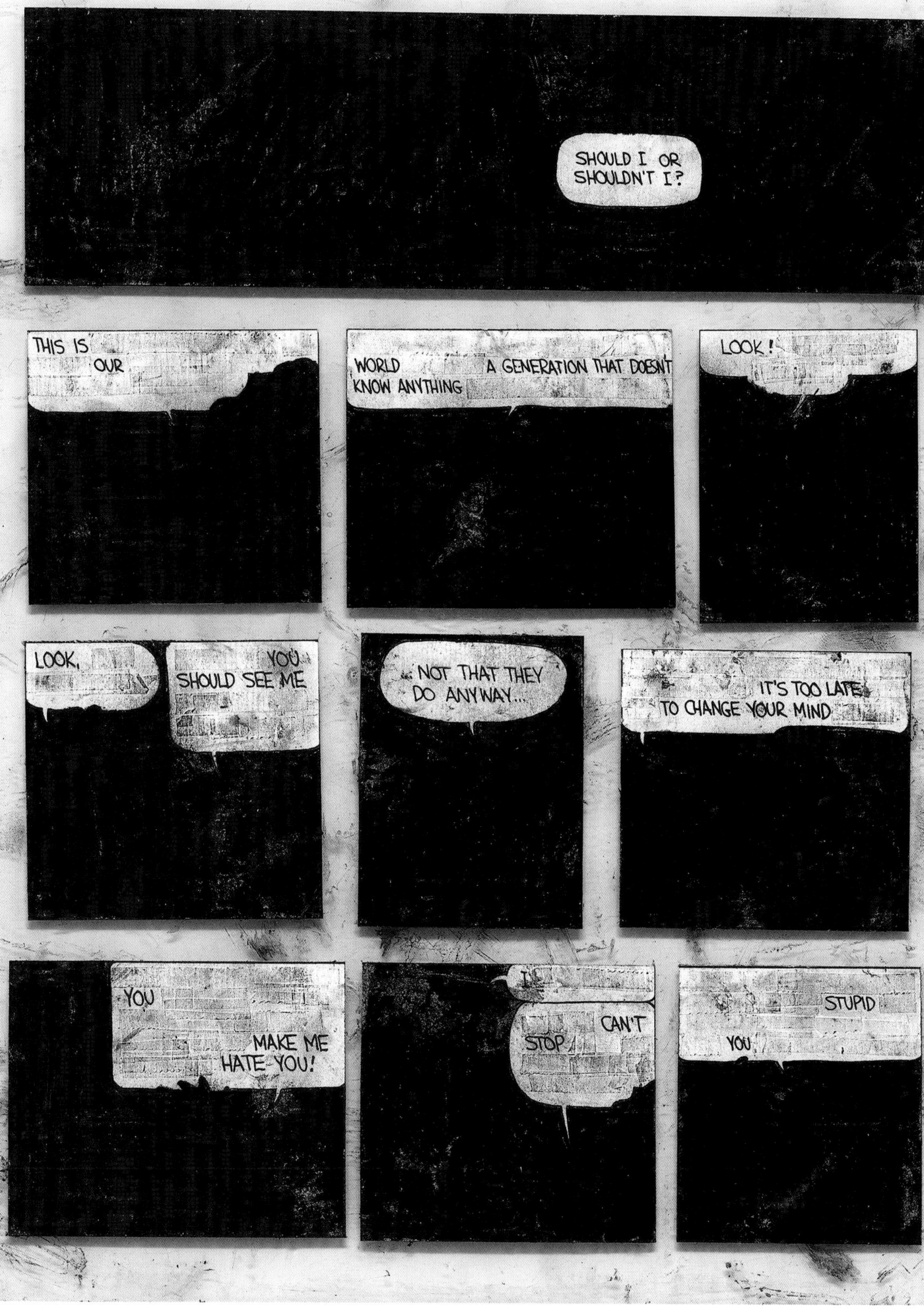
SHOULD I OR SHOULDN'T I?
THIS IS OUR
WORLD A GENERATION THAT DOESN'T KNOW ANYTHING
LOOK!
LOOK,
YOU SHOULD SEE ME
NOT THAT THEY DO ANYWAY...
IT'S TOO LATE TO CHANGE YOUR MIND
YOU MAKE ME HATE YOU!
I
CAN'T STOP
STUPID YOU

Little

Maybe,
He can save a hideous blob of
People but

In the back of your
Mind you know you

Won’t be able to understand

It must be more about us than
you sicko!

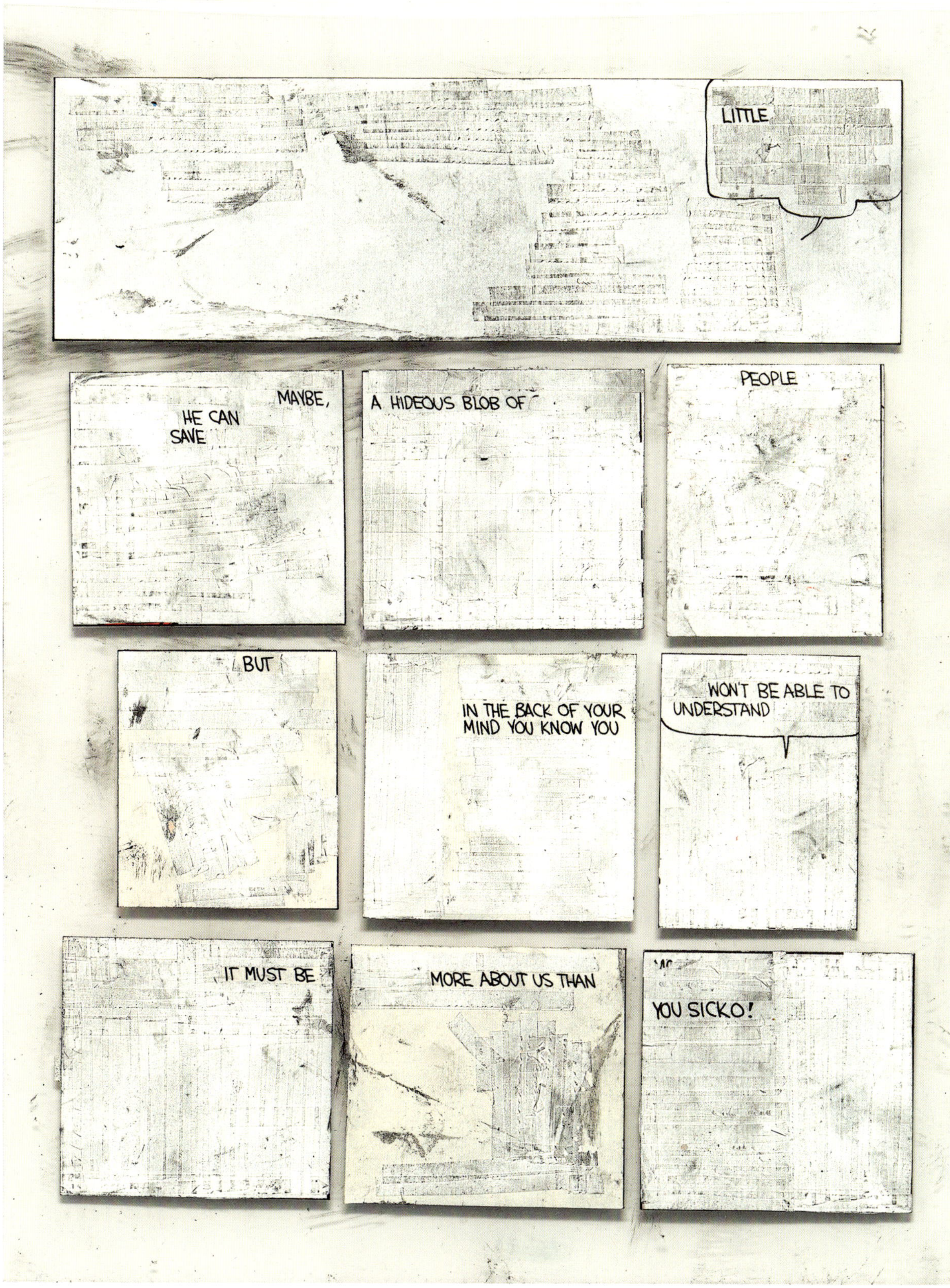
LITTLE
MAYBE,
HE CAN
SAVE
A HIDEOUS BLOB OF
PEOPLE
BUT
IN THE BACK OF YOUR
MIND YOU KNOW YOU
WON'T BE ABLE TO
UNDERSTAND
IT MUST BE
MORE ABOUT US THAN
YOU SICKO!

Idiot

Odd-colored boy
Makes me mad
He's playing
Or
Dreaming. Thing Calling
Madly,
Promising himself to better
Love! One's hideous
Nothing
And
Hope

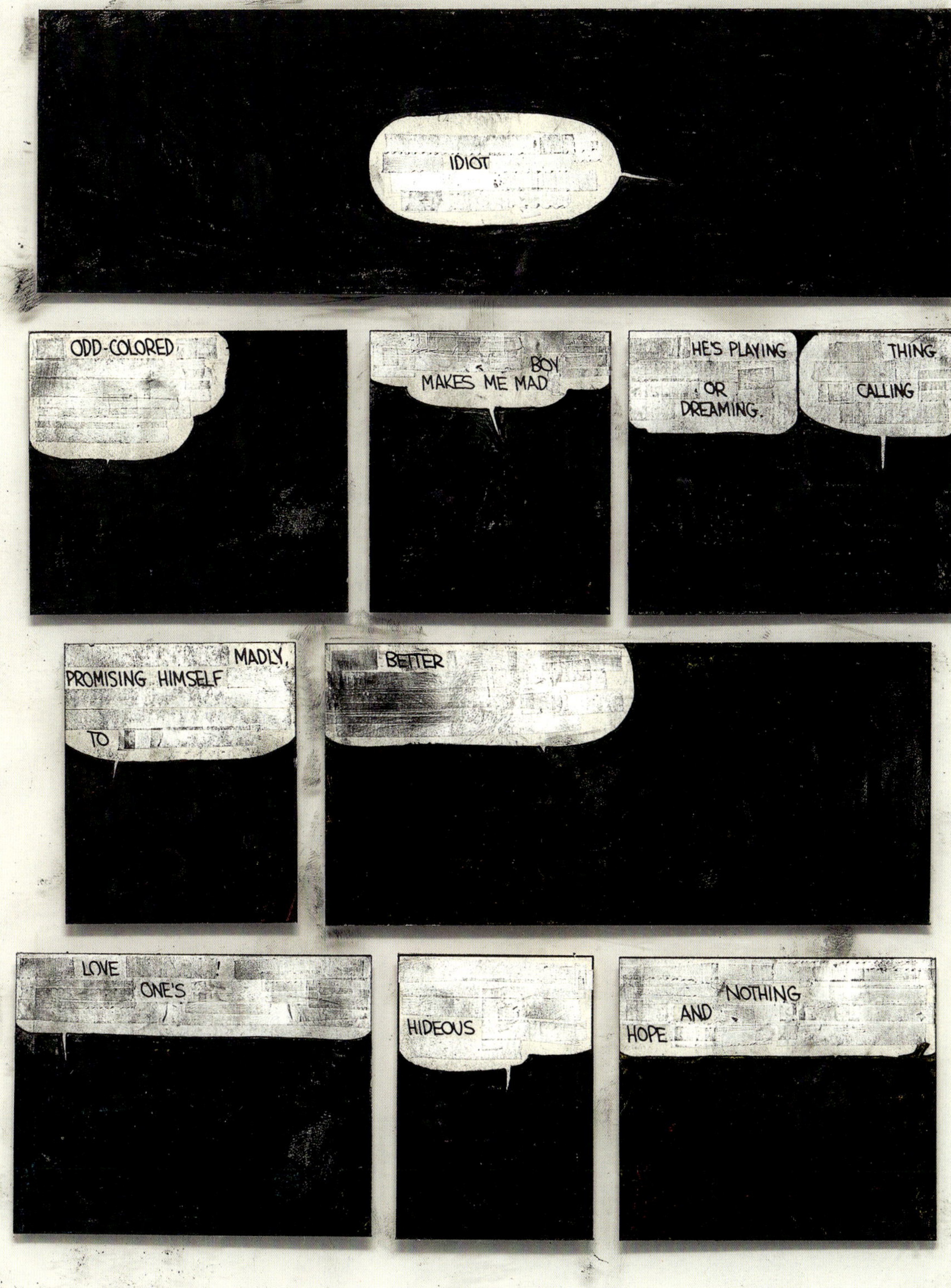
IDIOT
ODD-COLORED
BOY MAKES ME MAD
HE'S PLAYING OR DREAMING.
THING CALLING
MADLY, PROMISING HIMSELF TO
BETTER
LOVE ! ONE'S
HIDEOUS
NOTHING AND HOPE

Come

Move

Move
This house is
Moving all the weird things

The dank
To escape! I can't hold on!

(Choke)

I'm over useless crashes
It never fails. This thing.

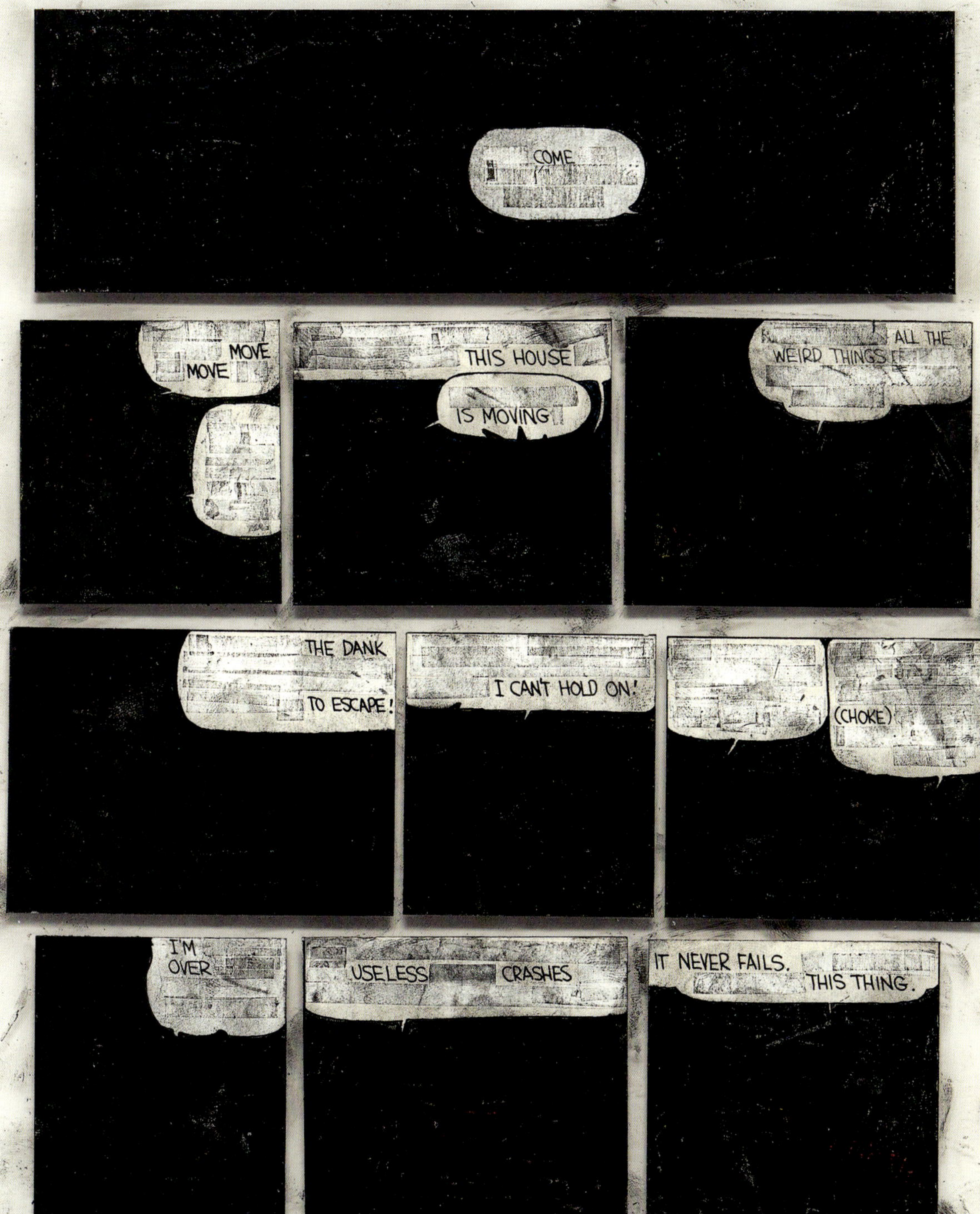
COME
MOVE MOVE
THIS HOUSE
IS MOVING
ALL THE WEIRD THINGS
THE DANK
TO ESCAPE!
I CAN'T HOLD ON!
(CHOKE)
I'M OVER
USELESS
CRASHES
IT NEVER FAILS.
THIS THING.

The Fire's Not Lighting

People Everywhere

It's beautiful to look
While we wait perfectly
He is nearly invisible no one will notice!

This moment we kill you
        We have a small, tasteless
Relief. You're the worm.

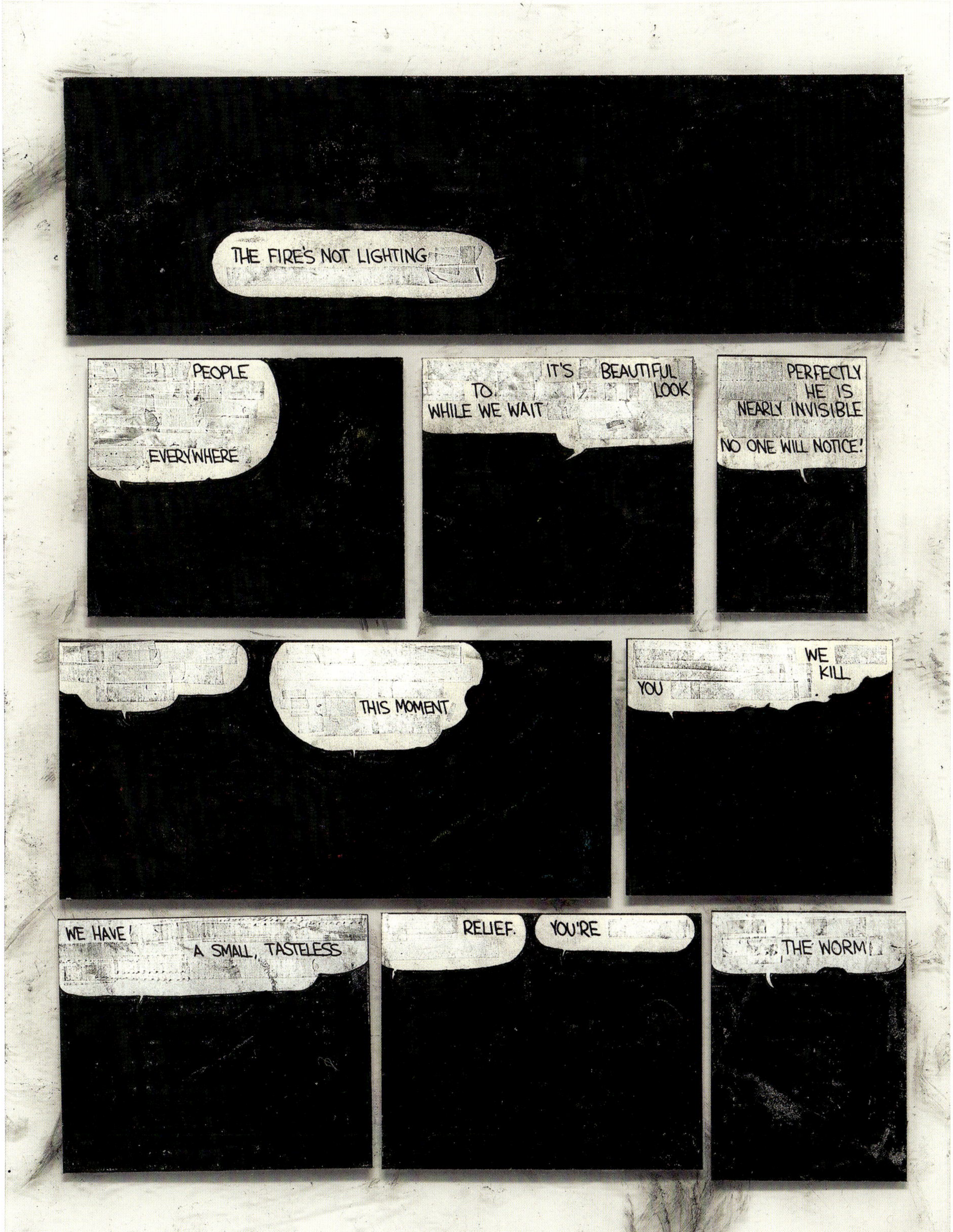
THE FIRE'S NOT LIGHTING
PEOPLE
EVERYWHERE
IT'S BEAUTIFUL
TO LOOK
WHILE WE WAIT
PERFECTLY
HE IS
NEARLY INVISIBLE
NO ONE WILL NOTICE!
THIS MOMENT
WE
KILL
YOU
WE HAVE
A SMALL, TASTELESS
RELIEF.
YOU'RE
THE WORM

The Dreaded

Something is different. But things haven't
Improved.   I'm
Disappointed. I think we'd better get
Out of history
We can be   Free
                        From the   monstrous
Boy, I
Face the prospect of never doing anything
If you're coloring

here

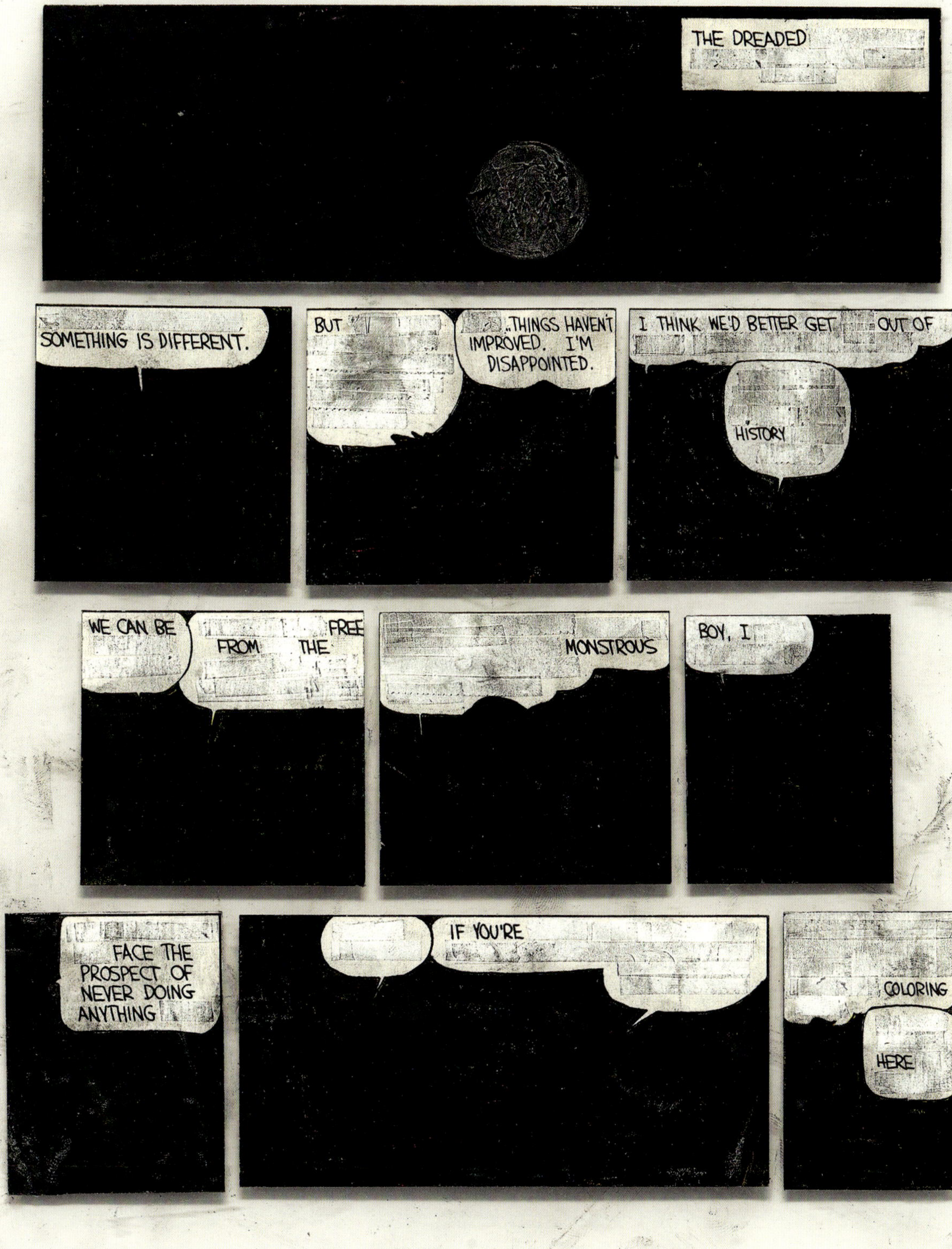
THE DREADED
SOMETHING IS DIFFERENT.
BUT
..THINGS HAVEN'T IMPROVED. I'M DISAPPOINTED.
I THINK WE'D BETTER GET OUT OF
HISTORY
WE CAN BE
FREE FROM THE
MONSTROUS
BOY, I
FACE THE PROSPECT OF NEVER DOING ANYTHING
IF YOU'RE
COLORING
HERE

CONTRIBUTORS

MELISSA CHIU is director of the Smithsonian's Hirshhorn Museum and Sculpture Garden, the national museum of modern and contemporary art. Since her appointment in 2014, she has advocated for contemporary art through the Museum's exhibitions, acquisitions, and public programs, with landmark exhibitions of work by some of today's most important artists. A native of Australia, Chiu earned her bachelor's degree in art history and criticism from the University of Western Sydney in 1992 and her master's degree in arts administration from the University of New South Wales in 1994. She completed her PhD with a dissertation on contemporary Chinese art at the University of Western Sydney in 2005. She has authored and edited several books and catalogues on contemporary art and has lectured at Harvard, Yale, Columbia, the Museum of Modern Art, and other universities and museums.

THEASTER GATES (b. 1973) is an artist and social innovator who lives and works in Chicago. Over the past decade, Gates has demonstrated the intricacy of Blackness through space theory and land development, sculpture, and performance. Through the expansiveness of his approach as a thinker, maker, and builder, he expands the role of the artist as an agent of change. Gates has exhibited widely. In 2010, he created the Rebuild Foundation, a nonprofit platform for art, cultural development, and neighborhood transformation that supports artists and strengthens communities. Gates is a professor at the University of Chicago in the Department of Visual Arts and serves as the special advisor to the president.

KARL HAENDEL is an artist who makes drawings, installations, films, and public projects. He received a BA from Brown University in 1998 and an MFA from the University of California, Los Angeles, in 2003. He also studied at the Whitney Museum Independent Study Program and the Skowhegan School of Painting and Sculpture. Articles and reviews on his work have been featured in the *New York Times*, the *Los Angeles Times*, the *Guardian*, the *New Yorker*, *Artforum*, *Frieze*, *Art and America*, and *Modern Painters*. His work was included in the Biennial of the Americas (2015), Whitney Biennial (2014), Biennale de Lyon (2013), Prospect (2011), and California Biennial (2004, 2008) and is in the collection of the Museum of Modern Art, Whitney Museum of American Art, and Guggenheim Museum, New York; Museum of Contemporary Art and Hammer Museum, Los Angeles; Fogg Art Museum, Harvard University; Kunsthalle Bielefeld, Germany; and Astrup Fearnley Museum of Modern Art, Oslo. He has received grants from the Pollock Krasner Foundation and the California Community Foundation and is represented by Vielmetter, Los Angeles; Mitchell-Innes & Nash, New York, and Wentrup, Berlin. He lives and works in Los Angeles.

BETSY JOHNSON is an assistant curator responsible for the photography collection at the Hirshhorn Museum and Sculpture Garden, where she has curated *Tony Lewis: Anthology 2014–2016* (2018); *The Evidence Room* (2019); *Feel the Sun in Your Mouth: Recent Acquisitions* (2019); *Ai Weiwei: Trace*, Skirball Cultural Center, Los Angeles (2021); *Toyin Ojih Odutola: A Countervailing Theory* (2021); *One with Eternity: Yayoi Kusama in the Hirshhorn Collection* (2022); *Rirkrit Tiravanija: (who's afraid of red, yellow, and green)*, Wrightwood 659, Chicago (2022); and *A Window Suddenly Opens: Contemporary Photography in China* (2022). She earned her bachelor's degree in integrative arts (1998) and her master's degree in art history (2004) from the Pennsylvania State University and is ABD in the department of art history and archaeology at the University of Maryland.

TONY LEWIS (b. Los Angeles, California, 1986; lives and works in Chicago), in his ever-expanding engagement with drawing, harnesses the medium of graphite powder to confront social and political topics such as race, power, communication, and labor. His work has been the subject of numerous museum exhibitions, including at the Aspen Art Museum, Colorado; Hirshhorn Museum and Sculpture Garden, Washington, DC; Institute of Contemporary Art, Philadelphia; Modern Institute, Glasgow; Museo Marino Marini, Florence; Museum of Contemporary Art, Chicago; Museum of Contemporary Art Cleveland; and Studio Museum Harlem and Whitney Museum of Contemporary Art, New York. He participated in the 2014 Whitney Biennial and received the 2017–2018 Ruth Ann and Nathan Perlmutter Artist-in-Residence Award at the Rose Art Museum, Brandeis University, Waltham, Massachusetts. Recent group exhibitions include *Minimalism-Maximalism-Mechanissmmm*, curated by Jacob Fabricius at the Art Sonje Center, Seoul, Korea (2022); *Grain of a Hand*, curated by Isabel Casso at the Museum of Contemporary Art, Chicago (2022); and *In These Truths*, curated by Edreys Wajed, Aitina Fareed-Cooke, and Aaron Ott at the Albright-Knox Art Gallery, Buffalo, New York (2022). Lewis's work is held in the permanent collections of the Albright-Knox Art Gallery; Dallas Museum of Art; Hirshhorn Museum and Sculpture Garden; Art Institute of Chicago; Museum of Contemporary Art, Chicago; Drawing Institute at the Menil Collection, Houston; Philadelphia Museum of Art; Hammer Museum, Los Angeles; and Museum of Modern Art and Studio Museum Harlem, New York.

CREDITS

Cover: Front: Tony Lewis, *Maybe*, from *Anthology: 2014–2016* (detail), 2015. Graphite, correction tape, and paper collage (comics) on transparency; 11 × 8½ in. (27.9 × 21.6 cm). Joseph H. Hirshhorn Purchase Fund, 2019 (2019.012.17). Photo: Alex Jamison. © Tony Lewis. Courtesy of Tony Lewis Studio and MASSIMODECARLO. (See pages 90–91.) *Back:* Tony Lewis, *Untitled (Yellow)*, 2020. Graphite, pencil, and colored pencil on paper; 72 × 96 in. (182.9 × 243.8 cm). Photo: Tony Lewis Studio. © Tony Lewis. Courtesy of Tony Lewis Studio

Interior: Pages 4, 13, 16, 46: Photos: Chenée Lewis. *8:* Photo: Genevieve Hanson. *12, 15, 25, 32, 35, 48, 51, 54:* Photos: Tony Lewis Studio. *18:* Courtesy of the International Dada Archive, University of Iowa Libraries, Iowa City, Iowa. *22, 59–125:* Photos: Alex Jamison. Courtesy of Tony Lewis Studio and MASSIMODECARLO. *23:* © 2022 Lawrence Weiner / Artists Rights Society (ARS), New York. Courtesy of Art Institute of Chicago. *26, 29:* Photos: Tony Prikryl. Courtesy of Aspen Art Museum, Colorado. *28:* Photo: Lee Stalsworth. © Glenn Ligon. Courtesy of the artist, Hauser & Wirth, New York, Regen Projects, Los Angeles, Thomas Dane Gallery, London, and Galerie Chantal Crousel, Paris. *41–45:* Courtesy of Karl Haendel and Vielmetter, Los Angeles. *47:* Photo: Heather Rasmussen. Courtesy of the artist and Blum & Poe, Los Angeles/New York/Tokyo. *49:* Photo: Robert Chase Heishman

COLOPHON

Tony Lewis: Anthology 2014–2016 was made possible with generous support from Theaster Gates.

First published in the United States of America in 2022 by:
Mousse Publishing—Contrappunto s.r.l.
via Decembrio 28
20137, Milan—Italy

In association with:
Hirshhorn Museum and Sculpture Garden
Washington, DC

For the Hirshhorn Museum and Sculpture Garden:
Director: Melissa Chiu
Deputy director: Jaya Kaveeshwar
Organizer of the volume: Betsy Johnson, assistant curator
Digital asset manager: Julia Murphy
Collections: Andrea Jain, Aimee Soubier
Senior editor: Laura Harger
Associate editor: Deane Madsen

For Mousse Publishing:
Publishing editor: Ilaria Bombelli

Edited by Laura Harger with Deane Madsen
Designed and typeset by Marcello Jacopo Biffi, Mousse Publishing

Printed and bound at Artigiana Grafica, Italy, not at government expense
26 25 24 23 22 1 2 3 4 5

ISBN 978-88-6749-514-6

Available through
Mousse Publishing, Milan
(moussemagazine.it)
DAP | Distributed Art Publishers, New York
(artbook.com)
Les presses du réel, Dijon
(lepressesdureel.com)
Antenne Books, London
(antennebooks.com)

We gratefully acknowledge the Native peoples on whose ancestral homelands our institution is located, as well as the diverse and vibrant Native communities who make their home here today. The Hirshhorn acknowledges that it was founded upon exclusions and erasures of many Indigenous peoples, including those on whose land it is set. This acknowledgment demonstrates a commitment to beginning the process of working to dismantle the ongoing legacies of settler colonialism.

HIRSHHORN
Smithsonian

This publication is dedicated to Greg,
who made it painfully clear that this was his favorite work of mine.
—Tony Lewis